BUILDING THE SUPERMARINE
SPITFIRE

BUILDING THE SUPERMARINE
SPITFIRE

SPEED IN THE SKIES

MARK A. CHAMBERS

The
History
Press

First published 2016

The History Press
The Mill, Brimscombe Port
Stroud, Gloucestershire, GL5 2QG
www.thehistorypress.co.uk

British Library Cataloguing in Publication Data.
A catalogue record for this book is available from the British Library.

ISBN 978 0 7509 6146 2

Typesetting and origination by The History Press
Printed in China

CONTENTS

ACKNOWLEDGEMENTS

Numerous individuals deserve great thanks for providing crucial support for the completion of this book. First and foremost, great thanks go to my loving family – wife Lesa, daughter Caitlyn, and sons Patrick and Ryan – for tolerating my ceaseless words of enthusiasm and providing encouragement and support for this project. My thanks also go to David Pfeiffer (civil records archivist), Nate Patch (military records archivist) and the entire staff of the Textual Reference Branch, and Holly Reed and the entire staff of the Still Pictures Branch, of the US National Archives and Records Administration (NARA) at College Park, Maryland. In addition, thanks go to Archie DiFante and Tammy T. Horton of the Air Force Historical Research Agency (AFHRA) at Maxwell AFB, Alabama, for providing additional research assistance and materials. Great thanks to Amy Rigg, transport commissioning editor at The History Press, UK, for her unwavering and fantastic encouragement and support in seeing this project through to publication. Finally, many thanks to the team at The History Press – including Christine McMorris and Andrew Latimer – for all their hard work on this book.

INTRODUCTION

The design and development of the Supermarine Spitfire, one of the Second World War's greatest air superiority fighters, is truly one of the most remarkable stories in aviation history. The unique sleek design of the Spitfire was truly a thing of aerodynamic beauty, forged with one matter in mind – speed. From unprecedented achievements in winning and setting new world speed records in the great Schneider Trophy races of the late 1920s and early 1930s to being rolled out for eventual aerial combat in one of the world's most tumultuous and destructive conflicts, the Second World War, the Supermarine Spitfire served as a 'game changer' in the struggle to control the skies.

The progressive development of the various marks of the Spitfire were intended to counter and outmatch a German aerial threat over England or in the European theatre at the time of the development of each specific Spitfire mark. The Spitfire Mk1 was designed to outperform, in terms of speed and manoeuvrability, the German Messerschmitt Me 109 Emil, developed in Augsburg, Bavaria, in 1935. The Me 109 held the world's speed record prior to the rollout of Britain's soon to be legendary Spitfire.

Seeking to outmatch more advanced versions of Germany's Bf 109, namely the F and early G series, in terms of firepower, Supermarine converted several Spitfire Mk1s into Mk5bs by adding two cannon to the four existing machine guns in the wings.

In 1941, Germany conducted numerous nuisance high-altitude photo reconnaissance missions over England in cockpit and cabin-pressurised Junkers Ju 86P bombers. To counter this threat, Supermarine developed the Spitfire Mk7 high-altitude interceptor variant, outfitted with extended wingtips for enhanced lift as well as a pressurised cockpit. When Germany introduced the excellent Focke-Wulf Fw 190A 'Butcher Bird' into battle over the English Channel and occupied France in 1942, Britain and Supermarine responded by developing the Spitfire Mk9, which outperformed the Fw 190A in almost every category of aerial performance.

The development of the fighter and photo reconnaissance variants of the Supermarine Spitfire was truly an Anglo-American effort. This fact became evident in the application of aerofoil technologies incorporated in the designs of the aircraft as well as in the developmental flight testing and carrier suitability testing of the Spitfires and navalised versions of the Spitfire, known as Seafires.

A total of 20,351 Spitfires were built, one of the world's most prolific mass-produced fighter aircraft during the Second World War. The following Spitfire design and development story also describes the tremendous combat effectiveness of this wonderful fighter aircraft that, together with the Hawker Hurricane, turned back massive German Luftwaffe bomber fleets from devastating England during one of the greatest air battles of the Second World War, the Battle of Britain. Throughout the Second World War, the Spitfire's mastery of the skies and its opposition was demonstrated on countless occasions, sweeping the skies clean of Axis threats. A total of fifty-five refurbished Spitfires still grace the skies in flight today.

1

R.J. MITCHELL AND THE SUPERMARINE AIRCRAFT WORKS LTD

PERSONAL HISTORY OF R.J. MITCHELL

The Supermarine Spitfire was the brainchild of the brilliant British aeronautical engineer Reginald Joseph (R.J.) Mitchell. R.J. Mitchell was born on 20 May 1895, in Butt Lane, Kidsgrove, Staffordshire, England. He attended Hanley High School during his early teens and exited school when he was 16. Young R.J. found work in the form of an apprenticeship at a train manufacturing firm – Kerr Stuart & Co. of Fenton. Mitchell produced drawings for the firm while attending night school, where he majored in mathematics and engineering.

R.J. Mitchell landed his first major job at the Supermarine Aviation Works in Southampton in 1917. He rapidly rose through the corporate ranks at Supermarine and became the company's chief designer in 1919. By 1920, he had risen to the position of chief engineer. In 1927, he became Supermarine's technical director.

Mitchell designed numerous flying boats, but his best design work came in the form of the sleek Supermarine S5 and S6 seaplane racers that took the great Schneider Trophy seaplane races, held in Europe during the latter 1920s and 1931, by storm and shattered world speed records both during and following some of the races. Design, development and flight experience with these revolutionary speed phenoms directly contributed to the design and development of Mitchell's greatest design achievement, the Supermarine Spitfire Mk1 prototype (K5054).

Reginald Joseph (R.J.) Mitchell, British aeronautical engineer and designer of the Supermarine Spitfire Mk1 prototype (K5054). (Royal Air Force)

Mitchell's love life blossomed in 1918, when he married Florence Dayson. R.J. and Florence's marriage produced their only child, son Gordon, in 1920. R.J. worked hard at his profession and, unfortunately, endured a tremendous amount of stress during his life, causing him to smoke quite heavily to help relieve the stress. Tragically, he would ultimately fall victim to the 'cancer stick', suffering two bouts of cancer that had spread to his rectum. He suffered the first bout of rectal cancer in 1933, but managed to maintain his steady work on the Spitfire, as well as a heavy bomber that became known as the Type 317. His resilience was tremendous, participating in flight training sessions and obtaining a pilot's licence in July 1934. He suffered his second and final bout of rectal cancer in 1936. The illness became so intense that he was forced to resign from his position at Supermarine in early 1937. He was truly blessed in that he was able to observe the flight testing of his Supermarine Spitfire Mk1 prototype (K5054), but sadly passed away on 11 June 1937. Mitchell was only 42 at the time, much too young for a great aviation visionary and pioneer.

OVERVIEW OF THE SUPERMARINE AVIATION WORKS LTD AT SOUTHAMPTON

The Supermarine Aviation Works Ltd was established in 1912 in Woolston, located within Southampton. Supermarine's first product was a flying boat that was displayed at the Aero Exhibition, Olympia, in 1913. His Majesty King George V was present at the exhibition and was impressed by the seaplane's design. Experimental aircraft design efforts were maintained throughout the First World War, but the firm also took on the important responsibilities of performing aircraft repairs and manufacturing to support Britain's war effort. In 1919, Supermarine produced the sturdy Channel Type Flying Boat, which featured a 240hp Puma engine and was an aerodynamically sound seaplane design. This seaplane design became synonymous with the Supermarine slogan, 'Not an aeroplane which floats, but a boat which flies.'[1]

Channel Type Flying Boats were later employed as airliners ferrying air travellers from England to France and from France back to England. In 1921, Supermarine rolled out their Seal reconnaissance amphibian flying boat, designed by Supermarine Chief Engineer R.J. Mitchell. The Seal possessed shipboard operational capability and could even be based aboard aircraft carriers. William Knight, technical assistant in Europe for NACA (The National Advisory Committee for Aeronautics – the predecessor organisation to today's National Aeronautics and Space Administration, NASA, in the

The Supermarine Seal reconnaissance amphibian flying boat, designed by R.J. Mitchell. (US National Archives, College Park, Maryland, Textual Reference Branch)

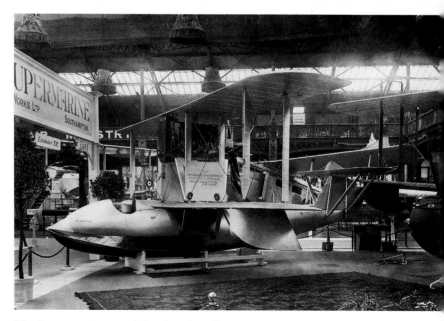

The Supermarine Sea King fighter flying boat, designed by R.J. Mitchell, on display at an international aviation exposition held in Europe. (US National Archives, College Park, Maryland, Textual Reference Branch)

USA), whose job was to report on the status and technical progress of aviation in Europe, provided an excellent technical summary of the Seal in one of his technical reports back to NACA headquarters in Washington DC:

The 'Seal' is a biplane flying boat with a flexible hull of circular section with two steps, the forward one of which is divided into eight water-tight compartments. The hull accommodates three people: a pilot in the nose, through which protrudes a Vickers machine gun, and a radiator operator and gunner in a large cockpit behind the lower plane. The amphibian gear is a slight modification of that used on the Supermarine in the Air Ministry Competition, September, 1920. The arresting or holding down gear is attached to the axle tubes. The wings fold rearward and have two pairs of streamlined steel struts on each side of the centre section. Ailerons are fitted to both planes. There is a float under each outer pair of interplane struts. The monoplane tail is raised considerably above the hull and the stabiliser and elevators are of the 'negative lift' type, being flat on the upper surface and cambered on the lower. The purpose of this is, of course, to prevent a sudden change of longitudinal trim in the case of engine stoppage. The rudder is balanced and there is a small fin forward of the balanced portion. A combined water rudder and tail skid is mounted on the bottom of the air rudder post.

A 450 HP Napier 'Lion' is placed midway between the planes in the centre section and drives a four-bladed tractor air screw. A large shuttered radiator is interposed between the engine and propeller. The engine is started by hand from the rear cockpit.[2]

In 1921, Supermarine rolled out yet another flying boat designed by R.J. Mitchell – the Supermarine Sea King, intended to serve the Royal Navy as a fighter. An advanced version of the Sea King, known as the Sea Lion Mk2, won the 1922 Schneider Trophy seaplane race held in Naples, Italy, in which a trophy was awarded to the winner of a race following a 212-nautical-mile course. The Schneider Trophy seaplane races were financed by Frenchman, Jacques Schneider.

In 1924, Supermarine rolled out yet another flying boat wonder, the Swan, designed by R.J. Mitchell. Only one Swan flying boat was produced and it saw airliner duty service with Imperial Airways in flights between England and France.

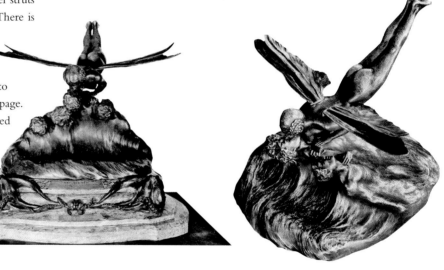

The Jacques Schneider Trophy. Left: front view. Right: top view. (US National Archives, College Park, Maryland, Still Pictures Branch)

Supermarine Swan airliner flying boat. (US National Archives, College Park, Maryland, Textual Reference Branch)

The Swan design spawned the highly successful Southampton flying boat. The development of this flying boat was directed by R.J. Mitchell. The Southampton was the largest flying boat design developed by Supermarine at the time, born out of a request from the Royal Air Force (RAF) for such an aircraft to fit the coastal defence and fleet escort/patrol roles. Supermarine unveiled the Southampton in 1925 and it remained in service for several years.

Southampton aircrews always spoke highly of their aircraft. The soundness and outstanding features of the Southampton design were promoted in the Supermarine corporate promotional literature displayed below.

The emergence of the Southampton enabled the RAF to test the fleet escort/patrol capabilities of the aircraft as well as refuelling procedures and capabilities at sea. In such an experiment, four Southamptons successfully completed a 10,000-mile cruise in the Irish Sea in September 1925. It should be noted with special interest that this successful cruise was completed in adverse weather.

In summer 1926, two Southamptons completed a long-distance voyage throughout the Mediterranean, journeying to Cyprus and numerous additional British maritime facilities. While these tests and experiments were carried out, Supermarine began the development and construction of all-metal Southamptons. Development and successful flight testing of the metal Southamptons gave the RAF the confidence to proceed with carrying out the world's longest formation flight, which resulted in the highly successful Far East Flight. As stated in Supermarine Aviation Works, Limited promotional literature:

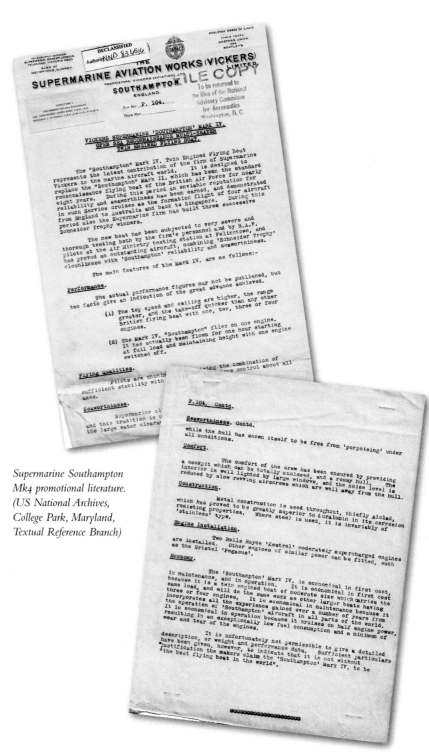

Supermarine Southampton Mk4 promotional literature. (US National Archives, College Park, Maryland, Textual Reference Branch)

Supermarine Southampton flying boat (production aircraft No. 1). The aircraft wears the Southampton town coat of arms. The highly successful Southampton was designed and produced in only seven and a half months. (US National Archives, College Park, Maryland, Textual Reference Branch)

The flight left Plymouth harbour in formation on October 17th, 1927, under the command of Group Captain Cave-Brown-Cave, and the start was a most impressive spectacle. The story of their adventures is difficult to tell, for the simple reason that they had no adventures. So far as dangers were concerned, the cruise was as prosaic as that of a P. and O. steamer plying between Tilbury and Bombay. They were troubled by barnacles collecting on the hulls in some harbours, by tar oozing from fuel lighters and fouling their white hulls, and once by a faulty Primus stove. One or two of the crews now and again had slight attacks of fever, and when men had to clean hulls below the water-line they suffered temporarily from ear-ache. But of real troubles there were none. The Southamptons and the Napier engines behaved perfectly, and everything went according to plan. It was this which made the flight so tremendously impressive. It was the finest piece of organised flying which the world has ever seen.

The itinerary may be briefly outlined. The flight crossed France and Italy to Athens, and then southward to Aboukir. Alexandretta in Syria, was the next port, and the flight then passed overland above the desert until the Euphrates was reached. This overland crossing was not dangerous, because a Southampton can maintain flight for a considerable distance on only one engine. The regular course to Basra and down the Persian Gulf to Karachi was followed, but from there a new air track was followed. Previously no seaplane had ever followed the coast round the Indian Peninsula; so the flight blazed a new trail and reported on the suitability of the harbours along the coast for seaplane work. From Calcutta along the East Indies was again a fairly well-known route, but the coast of Australia had only once before been flown round by a seaplane. The Southamptons first flew down the west coast and after circling the whole continent returned to Singapore. From there they made another cruise to Hong-Kong and then returned to Singapore which is to be the permanent station of the flight.[3]

The all-metal Supermarine Southampton, piloted by Group Captain H.M. Cave-Brown-Cave, DSO, DFC, on the Far East Flight. A Far East Flight Southampton was proudly displayed at the International Aero Exhibition. (US National Archives, College Park, Maryland, Textual Reference Branch)

An RAF Far East Flight Supermarine Southampton in flight. (US National Archives, College Park, Maryland, Textual Reference Branch)

Other flying boats developed by Supermarine during the latter 1920s included the wooden Supermarine Jaguar Solent torpedo-armed flying boat and a passenger-carrying flying boat version. In 1928, Vickers gained control of Supermarine and produced the Sea Hawk flying boat.

In 1930, Vickers Supermarine had on its drawing boards a huge 'aerial ocean liner' envisioned as a competitor for domination of the world airlines market with the German Dornier Do X, which toured the world in 1929. The envisioned Vickers Supermarine 'aerial ocean liner' concept became known as the 'Geant'. Interestingly, the aircraft was to be powered by six engines and utilise elliptical wings, similar to those eventually used on R.J. Mitchell's famous Spitfire fighter. The Geant's wings, however, were to be much larger and thicker, capable of accommodating several passengers and having windows near the wing roots. The Geant was never produced. The concept, however, served as proof that the Supermarine team was exploring the use of elliptical wings in aircraft designs long before the Spitfire concept was conceived.

In the case of the Spitfire, Supermarine aerodynamicists were largely responsible for developing the elliptical wings used in the Spitfire design. As stated by Tony Holmes in his excellent coverage of the development of the Spitfire, in Part 1 ('The Battle of Britain: 1940') of the book *Dogfight: The Greatest Air Duels of World War II* (2013), 'Soon, the wing had taken on an elliptical shape, as aerodynamicists at Supermarine calculated that it would create the lowest induced drag in flight. Such a flying surface also meant that the wing root would be thick enough to house the undercarriage when retracted.'[4]

The wooden Supermarine Jaguar Solent passenger-carrying flying boat. (US National Archives, College Park, Maryland, Textual Reference Branch)

The wooden Supermarine Jaguar Solent torpedo-armed flying boat. (US National Archives, College Park, Maryland, Textual Reference Branch)

Vickers Supermarine Sea Hawk flying boat. (US National Archives, College Park, Maryland, Textual Reference Branch)

The German Dornier Do X moored in the waters of Hampton Roads, Virginia, in 1929. The aircraft was making an international visit to America. (US National Archives, College Park, Maryland, Still Pictures Branch)

The German Dornier Do X makes a water take-off from Hampton Roads, Virginia, in 1929. The aircraft had just completed an international visit to America. (US National Archives, College Park, Maryland, Still Pictures Branch)

The envisioned huge Vickers Supermarine Geant. (US National Archives, College Park, Maryland, Textual Reference Branch)

The German Dornier Do X in flight over NAS Hampton Roads (now Naval Station, Norfolk), Virginia, US, in 1929. (US National Archives, College Park, Maryland, Still Pictures Branch)

Opposite page: Artistic rendering depicting the Vickers Supermarine Scapa. (US National Archives, College Park, Maryland, Textual Reference Branch)

Right: Vickers Supermarine Scapa in flight. (US National Archives, College Park, Maryland, Textual Reference Branch)

In 1932, a derivative of the successful Southampton, known as the Scapa, rolled off the Vickers-Supermarine assembly line. The Scapa, designed by R.J. Mitchell, served with the RAF in the coastal/anti-submarine warfare (ASW) patrol role starting in 1935. Another derivative of the Southampton, the Stranraer, also designed by R.J. Mitchell, was developed by Vickers-Supermarine during the mid-to-late 1930s and served with the Royal Canadian Air Force in the ASW patrol role during the early years of the Second World War.

R.J. Mitchell's seaplane design success continued in 1935 with the introduction of the Supermarine Walrus amphibian, which served as a scout flying boat that could be operated from Royal Navy warships and was employed in the critical search and rescue (SAR) role during the Second World War.

Vickers Supermarine Scapa performing a water take-off. (US National Archives, College Park, Maryland, Textual Reference Branch)

Vickers Supermarine Scapa performing an overflight. (US National Archives, College Park, Maryland, Textual Reference Branch)

The Walrus amphibian was another Supermarine seaplane success story that proved its worth, performing the all-important SAR role during the Second World War. (Royal Air Force)

2

FEELING THE NEED FOR SPEED:

THE GREAT SCHNEIDER TROPHY SEAPLANE RACES OF THE 1920S AND EARLY 1930S

THE SUPERMARINE S4 SEAPLANE RACER IN THE 1925 SCHNEIDER TROPHY SEAPLANE RACE

In 1925, Supermarine sought to expand its influence in the global aeronautics arena by pursuing the development of a high-speed seaplane racer specifically developed to compete in the 1925 Schneider Trophy seaplane race held in the United States at Bay Shore Park, Baltimore, Maryland. This seaplane racer, designed by R.J. Mitchell, became known as the Supermarine S4. As stated in Supermarine corporate literature later produced in 1929:

The Supermarine Napier S4 seaplane racer preparing to taxi out onto the water at Bay Shore Park, Baltimore, Maryland, during the 1925 Schneider Trophy seaplane race. The aircraft had previously set a world speed record of 226mph. (US National Archives, College Park, Maryland, Textual Reference Branch)

This machine, a monoplane with a Napier racing engine, was a surprise to everyone. It was a cantilever monoplane of extremely clean design, but in every way unlike what had come to be associated with the name of Supermarine. For a few weeks it actually held the world's speed record over a three kilometre course. It was not, however, fated to be a winner, but it formed the basis for the design of the Supermarine Napier S.5, a low-wing monoplane, which scored first and second places in the Schneider Contest at Venice in 1927.[5]

The Supermarine S4 experienced catastrophic aerodynamic problems in flight and crashed during the race, opening the door to victory for the American entry, a Curtiss R3C-2 seaplane racer, piloted by none other than American aviation legend and later the Second World War hero, Lt James H. Doolittle.

THE SUPERMARINE S5 SEAPLANE RACER IN THE 1927 SCHNEIDER TROPHY SEAPLANE RACE

For the 1927 Schneider Trophy seaplane race held in Venice, Italy, R.J. Mitchell and the Supermarine aircraft design team developed a true aerial thoroughbred in the form of the S5 seaplane racer. The aircraft was specifically designed to top the world speed record set by Italy's Major Mario de Bernardi in his aerodynamically sleek Macchi M39 seaplane racer at the 1926 Schneider Cup seaplane race held at Hampton Roads, Virginia, in the United States. In the S5, Mitchell and his design team corrected the design flaws, namely an

First Lieutenant James H. Doolittle and his Curtiss R3C-2 seaplane racer, the eventual winner of the 1925 Schneider Trophy seaplane race, at NAS Anacostia DC, before the 1925 race held at Bay Shore Park, Baltimore, Maryland. (NASA Langley Research Center)

adjustment correcting a flutter problem that caused the demise of the S4 in the 1925 Schneider Cup race.

In the 1927 Schneider Cup race, the Supermarine Napier S5 took first and second place, stunning the world. As stated in Supermarine corporate literature, later published in 1929:

> Flight-Lieut Webster, AFC, in the winning machine, made an average speed of 281.51mph round the triangular course, and in course of doing so established a world's record for 100 kilometres. The same machine in November, 1928, flown by Flight-Lieutenant D'Arcy Greig, DFC, AFC, established the British speed record of 319.57mph [514.308km/h] over a three kilometre course, which is the greatest speed at which a human being has ever travelled.[6]

The technological achievement embodied in the design of the Supermarine Napier S5 was described in detail in a National Advisory Committee for Aeronautics (NACA) circular prepared by the committee's third technical assistant, John Jay Ide, in Europe in March 1928:

> As the winner of the 1927 race for the Schneider Seaplane Trophy, and as a potential holder of the world's speed record in the near future, the Supermarine S.5 with Napier 'Lion' racing engine is one of the most interesting of modern British aircraft, and it is with a good deal of satisfaction that we are able to place before our readers some particulars and a number of illustrations of its more interesting features. In his paper read recently before the R.Ae.S. & I.Ae.E., Mr R.J. Mitchell, chief engineer of the Supermarine Aviation Works, gave certain very interesting figures relating to the S.5, but owing to the fact that the results of wind-tunnel tests could not be published, much information which would

Italy's Major Mario de Bernardi disembarks from his Macchi M39 racer in the waters of Hampton Roads, Virginia, following the successful completion of a preliminary flight in prelude to the 1926 Schneider Trophy seaplane race. (US National Archives, College Park, Maryland, Still Pictures Branch)

The Supermarine Napier S5 at the 1927 Schneider Trophy race held in Venice, Italy. (US National Archives, College Park, Maryland, Textual Reference Branch)

A Supermarine S5 piloted by Worsley, in a heat with a Gloster IV piloted by Kinkead, during the 1927 Schneider Trophy race held in Venice, Italy. (US National Archives, College Park, Maryland, Still Pictures Branch)

have been extremely interesting had to be withheld. Nor are we, for obvious reasons, in a position to give these here. For instance, the proportion of the total drag represented by the fuselage, the floats, the float struts, and the wings. But in the absence of such information it is permissible to speculate a little and to attempt to form, from other sources, an idea of the efficiency of a seaplane like the S.5.[7]

★ ★ ★

When it is remembered that the machine is a seaplane, and that therefore the float landing gear must offer considerably greater drag than a land landing gear, this low value of the drag is very remarkable.

Concerning the features of design which enabled this low drag to be attained, Mr. Mitchell gave in his lecture, previously referred to, the main changes as between the S.4 and the S.5, and the gain in speed which he attributed to the various changes. As these figures were given in *Flight*, of February 2, 1928, it is not proposed to repeat them here. Figure 1 will serve to show how small are the frontal areas of fuselage and floats in the S.5, and these and other illustrations give an idea of the care taken in streamlining unavoidable projections, and in fairing the various surfaces into the fuselage. The brief specification at the end of these notes contains the main available data relating to the seaplane, and it is of interest to note that the 'Wing Power' is the highest of any plane ever described in *Flight*, being no less than 7.6hp/sq.ft [81.7hp/sq.m].

Constructional Features

Although in a pure speed seaplane like the S.5, the aerodynamic design is perhaps the more interesting, there are a number of constructional features which are somewhat unusual, and which were developed as a result of the special conditions to be met with in a high-speed plane.

The fuselage of the S.5 is built entirely of metal (Fig. 2), chiefly duralumin, and an examination of the photograph of the fuselage in skeleton will show that by using this material and making the body more or less a monocoque, a good deal of space was saved so that it became possible to keep the cross section down to a minimum. In fact, the pilot sits on the floor, and as his shoulders touch the metal skin of the fuselage the only space lost is represented by the thickness of the duralumin skin! The method of building up the fuselage is fairly clear from Figure 2. Closely spaced frames or formers of flat U-section give the form of the fuselage from point to point, while the skin is made to serve in the capacity of longerons, i.e., is a part of the stress-resisting structure, reinforced here and there by fore-and-aft stringers.

In the forward portion there are specially strong frames for the support of wing roots, landing gear struts and, at the top, for the attachment of the anti-lift wire bracing. The reason why the latter point is one of great importance in the design is that with the system of bracing used, this point serves to stabilise the bracing of the whole seaplane, floats as well as wings. The location of this 'key point' may be seen in Figure 6, and details of the fittings, etc., are shown in a sketch.

The front bottom portion of the fuselage is built up as an engine bearer, with two main bearers of box section secured to cradles. In this region, as well as between the spar frames, the duralumin plating is laminated so as to give extra strength, a maximum of three thicknesses of 18G. being required in places. With the scoop-formed engine mounting used, the engine becomes very accessible, as Figure 3 shows.

The two floats are also of all-duralumin construction with the exception of the center section of the starboard float, which is made of steel so as to support the main fuel tank, which is situated here. The floats are of the single-step type, and have single central longitudinal bulkheads to which are attached the transverse frames, spaced some 2 feet apart. A number of longitudinal members are fitted between the frames (Figs. 7 and 8).

The controls are of perfectly normal type, and there is no form of variable gearing except the slight amount introduced in the ailerons by the forward angle of the aileron cranks. In spite of this the seaplane is reported to be relatively easy to handle in so far as a seaplane flying at somewhere in the neighborhood of 300MPH can be called 'easy.'

Owing chiefly to lack of time in which to produce an all-metal wing, the wings of the S.5 are of wood construction. Doubtless a certain amount of experimentation would have had to be done therefore an all-metal wing could be produced, and to save time the well-tried and proved wood construction was adopted. The two wing halves of the seaplane are built on the normal two-spar principle, with ribs of normal type except for the somewhat unusually with flanges necessary in order to secure the screw fixings of the wing radiators. From the bracing wire fittings to the tip of the wing there is a diagonal member introduced, the function of which is to stiffen the wing tip against torsion and thus reduce the chances of wing flutter being set up (Fig. 4). The wing covering is $\frac{1}{8}$inch three-ply, and over this are placed the radiators which are of the wing-surface type and have a perfectly smooth exterior. The radiators form a large percentage of the metal wing surface, and when it is remembered that the average wing loading is 28lb/sq.ft., which may be increased to 2G. Far more during rapid turns, etc., while the local loading may in seaplanes reach a much higher figure still, it will be realised that to design radiators of low weight and yet subject to such great loads was no easy task. It is not possible to give details of the radiators ultimately evolved, and which gave no trouble whatever, and are divided into top surface and bottom surface units, the method of feeding them from the header tank being illustrated in Figure 9. The wing section is a biconvex (symmetrical) one of medium thickness.

Bracing of the wings is, as already mentioned, entirely by streamline wires, the top point of the fuselage deck fairing serving to stabilise the whole bracing system of wings and floats.

Gasoline, Oil and Water Systems

With a fuselage of such very small cross-sectional area, the subject of gasoline system, and also to some extent oil and water system, became somewhat of a problem. It was found that there would be no room in the fuselage for a gasoline tank, and ultimately it was decided to place the main tank in the starboard float. This has the advantage of lowering somewhat the center of gravity of the seaplane, and also the offset load on the starboard side helped to counteract engine torque both when accelerating on the water and in flight. The distance the gasoline had to be lifted was, however, such that although in normal straight flight the gasoline pump could handle it, during a steep turn, with centrifugal force increasing the virtual distance, the engine would be momentarily starved, and so a small service tank was placed in the fairing behind the starboard cylinder block. Thus during a turn the engine takes its gasoline from the small tank, the straight leg of the Schneider course giving the pump an opportunity of filling this tank from the float tank before the next turn was reached. The actual fuel system is diagrammatically illustrated in Figure 9. The gasoline capacity, by the way, is 55 gallons.

Not only because of the high speed at which the Napier 'Lion' racing engines were run in the Schneider Race, but also on account of the propeller gearing in the winning seaplane, which naturally called for efficient lubrication, bearing in mind that frictional losses in the gears must have amounted to a good many horsepower, the oil system of the S.5 required rather close attention, and the normal disposition was not regarded as being sufficient. Consequently, the oil coolers were arranged along the sides of the fuselage, where presumably they would be in the slip stream and always getting a good supply of fresh, cool air. Whether that position is the best possible is, perhaps, open to doubt, since it would seem likely that the air does not follow smoothly the surface of the fuselage but is considerably churned up and also already heated to some extent by passing over the engine. Be that as it may, that was the arrangement chosen, and in the geared-engine seaplanes further cooling of the gears was obtained by cutting openings in the cowlings over the cylinder blocks.

Right: A Supermarine S5 seaplane racer is revved up in preparation for the 1927 Schneider Trophy race in Venice, Italy.
Above: The winning Supermarine S5 at the 1927 Schneider Trophy race in Venice, Italy. The aircraft featured a streamlined all-metal fuselage. (US National Archives, College Park, Maryland, Textual Reference Branch)

The water system is, chiefly due to the use of wing radiators, somewhat unusual, although not by any means particularly complicated. The water header tank is in the fairing behind the central cylinder bank, and the water is led to the trailing edge first, there dividing into two branches, of which one goes to the up surface radiator and one to the lower surface. After passing through the radiators the water emerges at the inner end of the leading edge and thence to the engine.

The main characteristics of the S.5 which it is permissible to give are as follows:

Wing span	26ft 9in (8.15m)
Wing chord	5ft (1.525m)
Wing area	115sq.ft (10.68sq.m)
Weight fully loaded	3,242lb (1,475kg)
Wing loading	28.2lb/sq.ft (138kg/sq.m)
Gasoline (55 gallons)	380lb (172.6kg)
Oil (5 gallons)	50lb (22.7kg)
Pilot	170lb (77.3kg)
Everling 'high-speed figure' (metric)	24.8

For obvious reasons performance figures cannot be given. Some time in March the S.5 will be tested over Southampton Water over a measured course, when it is hoped that it will beat the world's record established by de Bernardi.[8]

And of course, the S5 did indeed top de Bernardi's world speed record in November 1928.

An S5 wing frame, which was resistant to torsion caused by flutter. Flutter caused the demise of the S4 in the 1925 Schneider Trophy race. (US National Archives, College Park, Maryland, Textual Reference Branch)

An S5 in various states of assembly at the Supermarine Aircraft Works Ltd at Southampton. Top: S5 engine assembly and fuselage. Middle: Side view of S5 fuselage and engine cylinder block. Bottom: S5 fuselage framework. (US National Archives, College Park, Maryland, Textual Reference Branch)

A close-up view of the tail of the triumphant Supermarine S5 in the 1927 Schneider Trophy race. (US National Archives, College Park, Maryland, Textual Reference Branch)

An S5 float in various stages of assembly. The aircraft's fuel tank was housed in the float. (US National Archives, College Park, Maryland, Textual Reference Branch)

THE SUPERMARINE S5 AND S6 SEAPLANE RACERS IN THE 1929 SCHNEIDER TROPHY SEAPLANE RACE

In September 1929, the Schneider Cup seaplane race was held at Calshot, England, and once again, one of R.J. Mitchell's engineering marvels stole the show. An advanced version of the S5, designated the S6, was specifically built to retain the Schneider Trophy for Britain. The S6 was truly revolutionary in that it was an all-metal design and more powerful and aerodynamic than its predecessor, the S5. Two Supermarine S6s (N247 and N248), assembled at Woolston, participated in the 1929 Schneider Trophy seaplane race. The S6s were flown by the RAF High Speed Flight. Flying Officer H.R.D. Waghorn successfully defended the Schneider Cup for England, flying N247 to victory. He achieved a top speed in the aircraft of 328.63mph. Unfortunately for England, N248 committed an infraction when its pilot performed an illegal turn within a marker pole and was disqualified. Nevertheless, the aircraft established new world records for 50 and 100km over the span of its flight. An S5 (N219), piloted by Flight Lieutenant D'Arcy Greig, also participated in the race, but came in third. An Italian Macchi M52R (No. 4) seaplane racer placed second in the race.

Britain's speed demons – the 1929 RAF High Speed Flight Schneider team. From left to right: Flying Officer H.R.D. Waghorn, Flying Officer T.H. Moon, Flt Lt D. D'Arcy Greig, DFC, AFC, Sqn Ldr A.H. Orleber, AFC, Flt Lt G.H. Stainforth and Flt Lt R.L.R. Atcherley. (US National Archives, College Park, Maryland, Textual Reference Branch)

A Supermarine-Rolls-Royce S6 at Calshot, England. (US National Archives, College Park, Maryland, Textual Reference Branch)

The S5, piloted by Flt Lt Greig, heads out on the course. An Italian Macchi M67 (No. 10), flown by Lt Monti, can be seen aboard the transport vessel. (US National Archives, College Park, Maryland, Textual Reference Branch)

Waghorn and his S6 in tow following flight trials. (US National Archives, College Park, Maryland, Textual Reference Branch)

A close-up view of the propeller and powerful Rolls-Royce 'R' engine. (US National Archives, College Park, Maryland, Textual Reference Branch)

A Supermarine Rolls-Royce S6, piloted by Flt Lt Atcherley, heads out on flight trials at Calshot, England. (US National Archives, College Park, Maryland, Textual Reference Branch)

A Supermarine S6, featuring the powerful Rolls-Royce 'R' engine, at the 1929 Schneider Trophy seaplane race. (US National Archives, College Park, Maryland, Textual Reference Branch)

Top: The Supermarine Rolls-Royce S6 being carted to the waterfront at Calshot, England.
Centre: The Supermarine S6 is pushed into the water.
Below: The S6 in tow. (US National Archives, College Park, Maryland, Textual Reference Branch)

Another view of the S6 at the 1929 Schneider Trophy seaplane race. (US National Archives, College Park, Maryland, Textual Reference Branch)

A Supermarine Rolls-Royce S6 is shipped to the starting point at the 1929 Schneider Trophy seaplane race on a specially designed transport vessel. (US National Archives, College Park, Maryland, Textual Reference Branch)

An S6 is transported to the race course aboard a specially designed pontoon boat. (US National Archives, College Park, Maryland, Textual Reference Branch)

A Supermarine Rolls-Royce S6A with 'R' type engine visible. The S6s that participated in the 1929 Schneider Trophy Race were re-designated as S6As following the race. (US National Archives, College Park, Maryland, Textual Reference Branch)

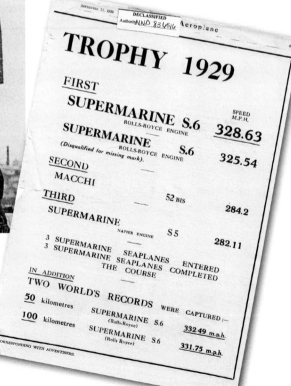

SEPTEMBER 11, 1929 ~ DECLASSIFIED Authority NND 834614 ~ The Aeroplane

681

TROPHY 1929

		SPEED M.P.H.
FIRST		
SUPERMARINE ROLLS-ROYCE ENGINE	**S.6**	**328.63**
SUPERMARINE (Disqualified for missing mark). ROLLS-ROYCE ENGINE	**S.6**	325.54
SECOND		
MACCHI	52 BIS	284.2
THIRD		
SUPERMARINE NAPIER ENGINE	S 5	282.11

3 SUPERMARINE SEAPLANES ENTERED
3 SUPERMARINE SEAPLANES COMPLETED THE COURSE

IN ADDITION
TWO WORLD'S RECORDS WERE CAPTURED :-

| **50** kilometres | **SUPERMARINE S.6** (Rolls-Royce) | 332.49 m.p.h. |
| **100** kilometres | **SUPERMARINE S.6** (Rolls-Royce) | 331.75 m.p.h. |

CORRESPONDING WITH ADVERTISERS.

The official 1929 Schneider Trophy seaplane race results as they appeared in The Aeroplane, *11 September 1929. (US National Archives, College Park, Maryland, Textual Reference Branch)*

THE SUPERMARINE S5, S6A, AND S6B SEAPLANE RACERS IN THE 1931 SCHNEIDER TROPHY SEAPLANE RACE

For the 1931 Schneider Trophy seaplane race, held once again at Calshot, England, but this time with only British competitors, R.J. Mitchell's finest developed seaplane design, an advanced version of the S6 (now redesignated S6A) known as the S6B, dominated its all-British competition, earning Mitchell the remarkable and unprecedented distinction of having designed all three of Britain's victorious seaplane racers for three consecutive Schneider Trophy Seaplane Races (1927, 1929 and 1931). Flight Lt John N. Boothman, flying S6B S1595, achieved a speed of 340.08mph in route to winning the contest. Seventeen days after the race, another S6B (S1596), flown by Flt Lt George Stainforth, attained a speed of 407.5mph, shattering the world air speed record.

The NACA's John J. Ide paid a visit to the 1931 contest at Calshot in September and provided a revealing description of events and their importance to the advancement of aeronautics in three detailed reports (one on the race and two on the development of the S6B) back to NACA headquarters in Washington DC:

The 1931 RAF High Speed Flight Schneider Trophy race team pose for a publicity photo in front of a Supermarine S6B seaplane racer. From left to right: Flt Lt E.J.L. Hope, Lt R.L. 'Jerry' Brinton (Fleet Air Arm), Flt Lt Freddy Long, Flt Lt George Stainforth, Sqn Ldr A.H. Orlebar (Flight Commander), Flt Lt John Boothman, Flying Officer Leonard Snaith, and Flt Lt W.F. Dry (Engineering Officer). (Royal Air Force)

Due to the last moment withdrawals of the Italian and French teams from the final contest for the Schneider Trophy, visits to the Calshot air station lost much of their interest from the technical standpoint.

The Italian Macchi-Fiat challengers were of a most novel design, the two engines being mounted in tandem in the nose, the drive from the rear engine being transmitted by gears through a shaft placed in the V of the forward engine to the front where two propellers placed close to each other turned on a common axis in opposite directions. The object of this propeller arrangement which, although used in marine torpedoes is novel in aircraft work, is of course to overcome the torque during the take-off. This would have rendered unnecessary such expedients as having floats of different sizes or placed at different distances from the longitudinal axis [as in the Supermarine S5], housing the greater part of the fuel in the starboard float, etc. (Fig. 1).

It is tragic that the hopes founded on the new Italian entries were blasted by the fatal accidents which occurred with disheartening regularity on Lake Garda.

The only French 1931 racing seaplane in a fairly advanced state was the Dewoitine designed for the Lorraine 'Radium' 18 cylinder inverted W supercharged geared engine. This engine, intended to develop 2300hp, broke up on the test bed when more than 1300hp was extracted from it. The power plants built by Renault and Farman required months of additional work before they would have been ready even for serious test. Fearing last January that the new engines would not be ready in time, the Air Ministry asked Hispano Suiza to develop a supercharged engine as it was thought that the previous experience of this company in building racing engines would have expedited matters. This order was, however, not accepted.

In the final juncture, only the 1929 seaplanes were available and of these only two – a Bernard and a Nieuport, both with direct drive 1500hp Hispano-Suiza engines – were left after the accidents to Bougault and Lasne. It was at length decided not to send these as even if proper propellers had been available, they would have had no possible chance against the British entries.

As France and Italy formally entered the 1931 contest only last December, insufficient time was left for England to develop completely new designs. Indeed if Lady Houston had not made a donation of £100,000 the Trophy would not have been defended.

If more time had been available it is thought that the Supermarine Company would have brought out a design in which the engine was completely overhung and the inverted V struts joining the floats and fuselage (the cause of a certain amount of drag) were replaced by vertical struts from floats to wings.

In the circumstances, the Air Ministry ordered two seaplanes (known as the S.6.B) which are merely refined versions of the 1929 racers with the additional fuel capacity necessitated by the changed conditions of the Contest. It will be remembered that whereas in 1929 the navigability trials were held on the day prior to the race, this year they took place immediately before the actual 350km (217.5mi.) flight. It may be mentioned that the consumption at full speed is at the formidable rate of 1½ miles per American gallon.

The greatest advance has been in the float design which has vastly improved the performance when waterborne. These floats are 24 feet long (about three feet longer than those of the original S.6) but due to their improved aerodynamic design have actually less drag in the air than their predecessors. The extra float length is towards the rear and this combined with alterations in setting and contour has markedly diminished the porpoising and yawing tendencies characteristic of the 1929 model when taking off. In order to counteract the torque effect which transfers a load of 500lb from one float to the other, considerably more fuel is carried in the starboard than in the port float.

It will be remembered that in 1929 not only did water radiators cover the entire wing surfaces but additional coolers were placed on the floats ahead of the forward struts. The cooling area, however, proved inadequate and the engines had to be run slightly throttled during the race. This year the entire float surface above the water line (except for the fuel filling plugs and inspection panels) was devoted to coolers. As the radiators expand about half an inch when filled with water near the boiling point an elastic framework had to be adopted to prevent buckling.

As shown in some of the attached photographs, the oil tank is in the tail fin and top fairing, the oil passing through radiators extending the length of the fuselage sides (figs 2–12).

Among the interesting refinements are the static balances fitted to the ailerons and rudder to guard against the possibility of flutter.

Most of the changes (including new floats shorter than those of the S.6.B) were incorporated in the two S.6 seaplanes of 1929 which are now termed the S.6.A. One of these was crashed during the training period with Lieutenant Brinton.

The S.6.B as flown over the 1931 Schneider Trophy Course has the following characteristics:

Span	30ft
Length	27ft 9in
Height	12ft
Wing area	145sq.ft
Weight empty	4,550lb
Pilot	165lb
Fuel (135 gallons)	1,125lb
Oil (15 gallons)	150lb
Total useful load	1,440lb
Total weight	6,000lb
Wing loading	41.4lb/sq.ft
Power loading	2.6lb/hp

The wing area of the S.6.B is unchanged from that of the S.6 but as the total weight has been increased to about 6000lb the wing loading is now over 41lb/sq.ft. Not-withstanding the considerable increase in wing loading as compared with the 36.2lb/sq.ft of 1929 the take-off and alighting speeds have been but slightly increased. This is due partly to the slightly altered wing section and partly to additional lift afforded by the larger floats.

Although the 1931 Rolls Royce R engine is identical in over-all dimensions, cylinder size and compression ratio with the 1929 model, the output has been increased from 1900hp to 2300hp at 3200rpm. The special 'sprint' engine which has been developed for the final attack of the 3km record can develop 2600hp for a few minutes.

The weight is 1630lb as compared with the 1530lb of the 1929 model. On the test bed where unlimited cooling capacity is available almost 3000hp has been obtained.

The life of the 1931 Schneider engine at full power is only about five hours but the intensive work of the company has resulted in its ability to maintain 1900hp indefinitely if desired. When it is realised that this engine is a development of the 825 Buzzard engine having the same cylinder dimensions (6 x 6.6in bore and stroke), the magnitude of the achievement will be apparent.

Detuned to give only 1500hp this engine would be well adapted for application in some of the forthcoming really large flying boats.

The diameter of the Fairey propeller has been decreased from the 9ft 6in used in 1929 to 9ft 1½in and weighs 232lb. The pitch is stated to be 17ft 6in and the efficiency 92%.

Photographs are likewise enclosed of the two seaplanes used for testing water and air conditions during the training period at Calshot. One is a Fairey Firefly IIM single-seat fighter (Rolls-Royce Kestrel II) and the other is an Atlas (Siddeley Panther) (figs 13 & 14). The latter is of peculiar interest being fitted with the first all steel floats made in England. They, like the seaplane, are the product of Armstrong-Whitworth of Coventry.[9]

★★★

This Supermarine S5, used to win the 1927 Schneider Trophy race, was employed in the training role in preparation for the 1931 Schneider Trophy race at Calshot, England. (US National Archives, College Park, Maryland, Textual Reference Branch)

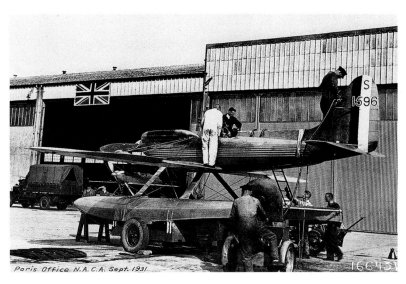

Performing an oil change for Stainforth's Supermarine S6B seaplane racer. The device in the foreground is heating the oil. (US National Archives, College Park, Maryland, Textual Reference Branch)

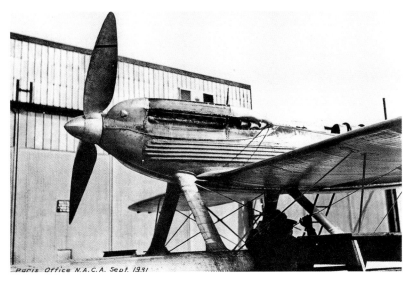

Close-up view of an S6B's front section with the engine camshaft cover visible. (US National Archives, College Park, Maryland, Textual Reference Branch)

Close-up view of an S6B's left aileron. (US National Archives, College Park, Maryland, Textual Reference Branch)

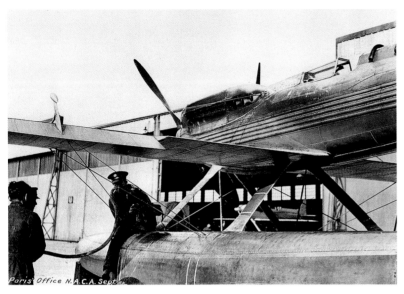

Fuelling up Stainforth's S6B. (US National Archives, College Park, Maryland, Textual Reference Branch)

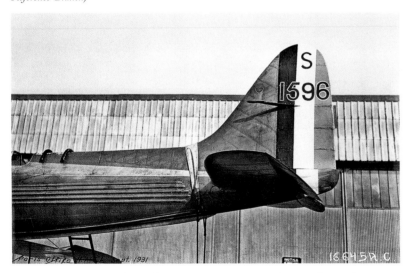

Close-up view of the tail of Stainforth's S6B. (US National Archives, College Park, Maryland, Textual Reference Branch)

A ground crewman removes the oil plug from the tail of Stainforth's aircraft. (US National Archives, College Park, Maryland, Textual Reference Branch)

Supermarine's fleet of S6 series seaplane racers awaiting tow to the starting point of the 1931 Schneider Trophy seaplane race. Left to Right: No. 7 S6B (Stainforth), No. 4 S6A (Snaith) and No. 1 S6B (Boothman). (US National Archives, College Park, Maryland, Textual Reference Branch)

Rear view of Stainforth's S6B seaplane racer. (US National Archives, College Park, Maryland, Textual Reference Branch)

An S6A (the 1929 Schneider Trophy winner), outfitted with a 1931 engine, modified floats and other refinements, is wheeled to the slipway at Calshot. (US National Archives, College Park, Maryland, Textual Reference Branch)

The S6B, flown by Stainforth, awaits wheeling out to the slipway before the 1931 Schneider Trophy seaplane race at Calshot. (US National Archives, College Park, Maryland, Textual Reference Branch)

A Fairey Firefly seaplane employed in the water and air condition monitoring role during flight trials for the 1931 Schneider Trophy seaplane race. (US National Archives, College Park, Maryland, Textual Reference Branch)

Stainforth's S6B is prepared for tow to the starting line of the 1931 Schneider Trophy seaplane race. (US National Archives, College Park, Maryland, Textual Reference Branch)

An Armstrong Atlas seaplane outfitted with stainless steel floats was also used in the water- and air-condition-monitoring role during flight trials for the 1931 Schneider Trophy seaplane race. (US National Archives, College Park, Maryland, Textual Reference Branch)

The Supermarine S.6.B seaplane, winner of the 1931 Schneider Trophy in the final contest, is a development of the S.6 1929 racer.

Before giving a description of the improvements in the 1931 racer a brief outline** [pamphlet issued by Supermarine Aviation Works Ltd] of the S.6 follows:

The Supermarine S.6 is a low-wing monoplane, twin-float type, built entirely of metal, the type construction being a development of the S.5.

The wing surface radiators are a new development. They are made as a wing covering taking torsional loads and consist of two thicknesses of duralumin with a very thin waterway in between. They have a perfectly flat outer surface and add no resistance to the machine. This method of construction has saved a considerable amount of weight over previous seaplanes.

The fuselage is constructed of metal, the skin taking practically all the stresses. The skin of the engine mounting takes all the engine loads. In place of the cantilevered engine mounting used on the S.5, the front float struts have been moved forward to provide a support and a substantial saving in weight has thus been effected. The floats are constructed of duralumin with the exception of the central portion, which forms the fuel tank which is made of steel. The duralumin is anodically treated to resist sea-water corrosion.

The bracing wires were specially streamlined. Six of the wires at present in the seaplane are only fitted as an additional safeguard during trials and practice, and will be removed for speed trials and racing.

As a result of the experience with the 1929 aircraft, the following improvements* (This article was prepared by the design staff of Supermarine Aviation Works Ltd, under the direction of Mr. R.J. Mitchell) were incorporated in the new 1931 aircraft, which are referred to as the S.6.B. type (figs 1–5):

1. Oil system (figs. 6 and 7) – This is, as before, housed entirely in the fuselage. Oil when it leaves the engine is forced along the side coolers to the top of the fin tank. By an arrangement of ribs and gutters the oil is kept in contact with the shell as it falls to the normal level and passes through a filter into the return (suction) cooler which is built on the same lines as the side coolers, but of greater section. Oil cooling had to be improved considerably to cope with the increased horse-power, and it was found that difficulty lay not so much in the transferring of it from the oil to the surface of the cooler. Eventually, as a result of extensive research work, it was found possible to increase the efficiency of the coolers by as much as 40 percent. This was done by sweating small vanes in the oilways, but a great deal of experiment was necessary before the type

and pitch of vanes could be decided, because excessive restriction in the flow increased the pressure difference between inlet and outlet by an enormous amount. The gutters in the fin tank performed a similar duty and the capacity of the tank itself was much increased to carry the additional oil required. In actual practice, the temperature drop between oil outlet and oil inlet reached 60° C, a figure never before approached on any aircraft.

2. Water system (fig. 8) – In order to keep the new engine at the correct temperature it was necessary to dissipate approximately 40,000 Btu of heat per minute from cooling surfaces. The efficiency of the wing radiators could not be improved to any appreciable extent and therefore more surface had to be provided. The topsides of the floats were accordingly covered entirely with radiator instead of the usual shell plating, and with this addition, cooling was adequate. A new type of header tank with a steam separator was designed to prevent any loss of water, but in other respects the system was unaltered.

3. Fuel system (fig. 9) – The fuel is carried inside the floats, and is delivered to a small pressure tank in the fuselage by means of engine-driven pumps. The engine is fed from this pressure tank. The fuel pumps cease to function on a steeply banked turn owing to the increased centrifugal loading when loads of five or six times gravity are experienced. The small pressure tank contains just sufficient fuel to keep the engine running during a turn, and is replenished when the pumps begin to work after the turn.

Considerably more fuel is carried in the starboard float than in the port float. This is arranged to balance the enormous engine torque, particularly at take-off. This effect is so important that it is doubtful if the seaplane could be taken off the water with a very light load of fuel as a result of the yawing effect produced by one float being loaded much more heavily than the other.

The effect of full engine torque is to transfer a load of about 500 pounds from one float to the other.

In the early stages of a good deal of trouble was caused by the transfer of the fuel from one float to the other, leaving one tank nearly empty while the other remained full, but this difficulty was in due course overcome by a special venting system in the overflow pipes from the header tank.

4. Floats – Extensive tests have been carried out on models both in the Vickers Experimental Tank at St. Albans, and in the wind tunnel at the National Physical Laboratory, to produce a form of float to satisfy aerodynamic and hydrodynamic requirements, in the most efficient manner. It has been found possible to reduce appreciably the air resistance per unit volume, and at the

same time improve the take-off characteristics when compared with the 1929 floats, both by reducing hump resistance and by increasing stability.

The method of construction of the new floats presented considerable difficulty owing to the fitting of water cooling radiators on the whole of the upper surface. The radiators expand nearly half an inch when filled with the cooling water at nearly boiling temperatures, and to prevent buckling of the skin an elastic framework construction had to be devised to take up the necessary expansion.

5. Control – The mass balances fitted to the ailerons and rudder were incorporated with a view to obviating any possibility of flutter developing (figs 2 and 4). On the S.5s slight aileron flutter was experienced if the controls were allowed to get slack. Calculations showed that at the increased speed of the S.6.Bs there was a possibility of trouble in this respect, and the mass balances were therefore fitted as a precautionary measure. When travelling at maximum speed, the ordinary small inaccuracies of construction make themselves felt by producing air loads upon the fin and stabiliser which necessitate loads upon the control column and rudder bar to correct. Since the tail unit is built into the fuselage, no change in rigging is possible. The elevators and rudder were therefore provided with small flaps on their trailing edges which were adjusted to the angle necessary to trim hands and feet off at top speed. These flaps were only a few square inches in area, but proved extremely effective in use. A curious point in connection with control on water was experienced this year. The new propellers were of 8ft 6in diameter, as compared with 9ft 6in for the 1929 aircraft, both types being designed by the Fairey Aviation Co. It was found impossible to take off with these new propellers owing to the fact that at an early stage in the take-off the seaplane swung violently to port even with full starboard rudder. It was, however, found that with the old 9ft 6in propellers the take-off was easy, and in fact, a great improvement on the S.6.As, owing to improved float design. Eventually, 9ft 1½in propellers were found to give satisfactory take-off, while with an 8ft 10in propeller, it was only just possible to get off under very favorable conditions.

★ ★ ★

Characteristics of the S6B Monoplane (from *The Aeroplane*, 30 September 1931):

Span	30ft
Chord	5ft 8in
Length overall	27ft 9in
Height	12ft
Wing area	145sq.ft
Weight empty	4,560lb
Pilot	160lb
Fuel (135 gallons)	1,125lb
Oil (15 gallons)	150lb
Weight fully loaded	5,995lb
Wing loading	41.3lb/sq.ft
Power loading	2.6lb/hp
Engine weight	1,630lb
Propeller weight	232lb

The 1931 R engine (fig. 10) used in this seaplane is a water-cooled twin-six type, developed from the 1929 racing engine (fig. 11) and from the standard 825hp Buzzard (H) engine (fig. 12). The bore and stroke are 6 and 6.6in, respectively, as in the Buzzard.

The Supercharger

The most apparent difference between the racing engine and the standard one lies in the superchargers. This is necessitated by the enormous volume of air drawn in by the racing superchargers. To avoid a very large diameter unit, air is taken into the rotor at both sides. The position of the air intake in the racing seaplanes has been chosen as in the V of the engine, to avoid the ingress of spray, and necessitating the sheet-metal air duct at the rear of the engine. This duct is utilised to compress the air a little before it reaches the carburetor [*sic*], and is retarded by the divergence of the duct before entering the carburetor [*sic*]. The reduction in kinetic energy produces a gain in pressure energy. This type of intake is now in use on many service airplanes.

The propeller reduction gear, of the straight-spur type is modified from the standard unit to conform with the airplane builder's requirements as to the shape of the nose. The camshaft and rocker covers are modified for fairing purposes. Beneath the engine the auxiliaries are raised a little on the racing engines to reduce the depth of fuselage required.

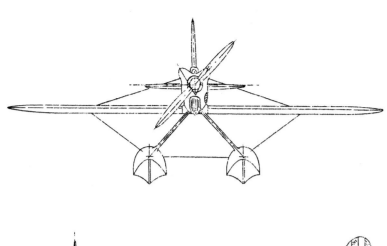

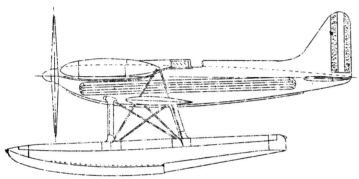

A two-view schematic (front and side view) of the Supermarine S6B seaplane racer. (US National Archives, College Park, Maryland, Textual Reference Branch)

A comparison of Supermarine S6 series seaplane racer engines and a conventional Buzzard engine. Note the increasing level of complexity of the Supermarine S6 series engines compared to the Buzzard engine. (US National Archives, College Park, Maryland, Textual Reference Branch)

Fig.10 1931 "R" racing engine used in S.6.B. seaplane

Fig.11 Rolls-Royce R engine used in 1929 race.

Fig.12 The standard 825 hp "Buzzard" engine.

The 1929 racing engine produced 1,900hp at 2,900rpm and weighed 1,530 pounds. The 1931 engine yields 2,300bhp at 3,200rpm and weighs 1,630 pounds. The power increase this year is 21 percent for a weight increase of 6 and ½ percent.

To obtain the 1931 performance, it was decided to raise the engine speed, raise the supercharger gear ratio, and increase the size of the air intake. The approximate power and speed were decided upon before commencing the development work to attain this performance combined with the necessary degree of reliability.[10]

★ ★ ★

How the Supermarine S6B was Built
[extract from *The Aeroplane*, 16 December 1931]

Through the courtesy of Mr. R.J. Mitchell at the Supermarine Aviation Works Ltd, we are able to give a general description of the internal structure of this seaplane and publish some pictures which will serve to give the world an idea of the way in which the Supermarine Works produced the fastest airplane in the world.

Everybody is familiar with the general layout of the seaplane as a low-wing wire-braced twin-float monoplane with a cantilever tail unit.

The Wings

The wings are of conventional two-spar construction with ribs spaced at 9½in centers. The entire surfaces, with the exception of the ailerons and rounded wing tips, are covered with radiators, which are screwed directly to the ribs and form the flying surfaces (Fig. 1).

The spars are built-up boxes of duralumin with channel-section webs which have outwardly-turned flanges. To these the flat strips which form the flanges of the spars are riveted. Each of the webs has a single longitudinal corrugation and this is flattened out at the points of attachment for fittings. The way this is done is interesting.

The superfluous amount of metal is removed by drilling two holes on the neutral axis and cutting slots of the proper width from one to the other. When the flanges have been flattened out this gap closes up. The material used is mainly 14G duralumin, but at points of localised stress in the way of fittings and the like the proper number of doubling plates are attached.

The reason for the angle at which the rear spar is inclined is that the stub spar is built into the fire-proof bulkhead, which has to be so slanted as to give adequate room at the rear of the engine.

The ribs consist of 16G duralumin diaphragms with flanged lightening holes. To the diaphragms are riveted flanges of extruded angle-section. The legs of the angle are of unequal thickness, one is 1/16in and the other 3/16. The latter is drilled and tapped to take the screws which hold the wing radiators in position.

The ribs are made in sections, as their flanges have to be flush with those of the spars. They are attached to these through vertical angle-pieces riveted to the webs of the spars before these are finally assembled. That is characteristic of these seaplanes, a kind of jig saw puzzle progress.

The inlet and outlet channels of the radiators necessitate the leaving of slots in the ribs, and this is achieved by dividing the diaphragm and joining the sections with small channel pieces. A similar arrangement is used at the nose, where a 10G strip is carried by such channels and radiators. These joints are finally covered with a capping strip attached in a similar fashion.

The wing-root fittings are attached to lugs on the stub spars by horizontal bolts and nuts. These fittings are of steel.

Each aileron moves between two shielding plates that form continuations of the upper and lower wing surfaces respectively and is operated by a push-pull rod that passes through the spar to an ordinary sort of bell crank.

The Wing Radiators

The wing radiators are built up from sheets of 24G duralumin arranged in pairs. The seams are made by riveting the sheets together with strips of Langite 1/16 thick between them. The sides of the radiator are ⅛ in. apart and this distance is limited by the means used to space the sheets apart (Fig. 2).

The radiators are attached to the wing structure by screws which pass through eyelets in the radiators and then pick up tapped holes or bosses in the wing beneath. When the radiator sheets have been drilled to take the eyelets they are separated and each hole is flanged with a special punch. When the sheets are put together again with the flanges facing inwards, the flanges butt up against each other and the eyelets when squeezed down make the whole joint water-tight. There is however, a certain relation between the gauge of sheet and the depth of flange, which can be made without cracking when the eyelet is pressed home. This relation limits the spacing of the sheets to ⅛ in.

The radiators are made with seams running fore and aft (parallel to the ribs), and these seams act as baffles so that the water has to flow across the wing and cannot pass diagonally from its point of entry to the collector pipe along the trailing edge.

The heaviest of the bracing wires is the front landing wire, which is of ⅝in diameter, the others vary according to the duties imposed upon them.

The Fuselage

The fuselage is a monocoque structure with 46 frames, or rather 'stations,' more or less equally spaced some 6 in. or 7 in. apart (Fig. 3). These are covered with duralumin sheeting (Fig. 4). One mentions this as it helps to give one some idea of the size of the engine bearers, which run from the nose back to frame 40 and form the only longitudinal members of the structure. The frames are mainly built from 18G strip and are of 'U' section with two outwardly turning flanges, to which the skin plating is fixed.

The engine bearers are of 14G duralumin, though necessarily strengthened by doubling plates at points of localised stress. Each bearer is of right-angle section, with the flanges bent back and shaped to fit the sides of the fuselage. The top flange of the angle is naturally kept for the engine feet to rest upon.

One might mention in this connection that whereas the fore-feet are bolted hard down, the rear feet rest in rubber pads and the holding bolts pass through slots in the bearers so that the engine can stretch itself as it warms up.

Between the engine and the cockpit is the sloping fireproof bulkhead with the water-header tank built into the top of the fuselage immediately behind it. The bulkhead is a sandwich of asbestos between the bulkhead proper and a sheet of duralumin fastened thereto. In spite of the numerous passages for pipes and controls which pass through it as well as a large inspection door, this bulkhead does keep a lot of heat away from the pilot.

The Fin and Oil Tank

At the tail the structure merges into the fin, which, together with most of the fairing behind the pilot's head, forms the oil tank and cooler. (Fig. 5.) This part of the structure has naturally to be oil-tight and is therefore built of tinned steal. The curious criss-cross of riveting which shows up so clearly in photographs of the tail unit is due to a large number of sloping gutters along the sides of the fin, so disposed that the oil, after being sprayed from the pipe at the top of the fin, is made to trickle down the gutters and over the internal structure, thereby ensuring that the greatest possible amount of oil is in contact with the metal all the time.

A similar purpose is served by the oil-coolers along the sides and belly of the fuselage. Those along the sides take the oil to the fin and that along the belly returns it to the engine. These coolers are shallow channels of tinned steel attached to the side of the fuselage.

They owe much of their efficiency to a number of tongues of copper foil athwart the flow of oil. These are soldered to the sides of the cooler and project at right angles into the stream of oil. They are staggered in such a way that the flow of the oil is not too seriously impeded. (Fig. 6.)

Control Surfaces

The rudder is built like the ailerons and is operated by cables attached to a lever inside the tail fairing and carried by an extension shaft bolted to the rudder spar. Into the rudder is built the trailing-edge strip of duralumin, which proved so useful for adjusting trim at full speed.

The stabiliser spars are built into the fuselage structure with ribs of conventional pattern. The whole has a riveted-on skin of light gauge duralumin sheet.

The elevators are built like the ailerons and are operated by a lever inside the fuselage. The elevator spars are formed by closing a channel with a leading-edge member of circular section.

An interesting feature of design is that the elevators are made to fit the fuselage as closely as possible. The ordinary cutaway used to clear the rudder movements results in an extremely poor streamline section at that part of the elevator. In the S.6.B this was avoided by ending the bottom of the rudder above the top limit of the elevators' travel.

The Floats

The floats have a mean reserve buoyancy of 57 percent and are carried by four T1 steel tubes. They are all 2in outside diameter, but the front pair are 8G and the after pair 17G. (Fig. 7.) At the top sockets of conventional pattern are used to hinge these to lugs on the fuselage. The front pair of struts also serve to support the engine mounting, to which they are attached.

At the lower end the tubes are built rigidly into the floats and pass through duralumin blocks through which they are bolted to the double frames. Where the tubes leave the floats they are naturally subject to very heavy loads in bending, so the tubes are stiffened against these stresses with a number of tongued sleeves.

In general conception the floats are conventional, though complicated to an inordinate degree by the fact that their middle portions are fuel tanks and their decking is formed by water radiators.

The fuel tanks were built to a full cross section of each float and have duralumin internal members with a tinned-steel skin. Where the internal frames come in contact with the skin tinned-steel angle pieces have to be used so that the rivets can be sweated over to ensure watertightness.

The rest of the float is built up conventionally with transverse frames stiffened by longitudinal. The bottom plating is mostly 16 or 18G duralumin.

This year for the first time water radiators were used to cover the entire floats above the chine line. These are built in the same way as those on the wing, but are in five sections to each float. This necessitates an intricate system of connections which are reached through handholes. (Fig. 8.)

These floats are a remarkable example of what can be done in the shops. The radiators could not be built to the floats, as both had to be made at the same time, so the former had to be built to molds. In spite of this, when the radiators were finally in position holes in the radiators picked up tapped bosses which had been sweated to the inside of the fuel tanks.

Anyone who has anything to do with building floats will realise at once the difficulties of working to limits demanded by such methods of assembly.

This brief account of the general structure of the Supermarine S.6.B does not attempt to describe in detail the actual manufacturing difficulties which must be overcome in building a racing craft of this type. It may, however, serve to show how Mr. Mitchell adapted the ordinary practice of aircraft engineering to produce the fastest seaplane in the world.[11]

The starboard wing frame of a Supermarine S6B. (US National Archives, College Park, Maryland, Textual Reference Branch)

The port wing water radiator of a Supermarine S6B. (US National Archives, College Park, Maryland, Textual Reference Branch)

The fuselage frame of a Supermarine S6B. (US National Archives, College Park, Maryland, Textual Reference Branch)

An S6B near full assembly. (US National Archives, College Park, Maryland, Textual Reference Branch)

The oil tank on an S6B. (US National Archives, College Park, Maryland, Textual Reference Branch)

An S6B float near complete assembly. Note the fuel tank located ahead of the step. (US National Archives, College Park, Maryland, Textual Reference Branch)

THE IMPACT OF THE GREAT SCHNEIDER TROPHY SEAPLANE RACES ON SECOND WORLD WAR FIGHTER AIRCRAFT DESIGN

The great Schneider Trophy seaplane races of the mid-to-late 1920s and early 1930s led to advancements in future fighter aircraft design. Valuable experience which had been accumulated in preparation for the races led aircraft designers to pursue the new fad in fighter design – the development of advanced inline engine, high-performance fighter designs. Consequently excellent designs, including the American Curtiss P-40 Tomahawk, Bell P-39 Airacobra, and North American P-51 Mustang, British Supermarine Spitfire, Italian Macchi C202 Folgore ('Thunderbolt') and Macchi C205 Veltro ('Greyhound'), were developed immediately prior to and during the Second World War. Some of these aircraft, specifically the Curtiss P-40 Tomahawk, North American P-51 Mustang and Supermarine Spitfire, played pivotal roles in affecting the outcome of the war.

The American Curtiss P-40B Tomahawk. (NASA Langley Research Center)

Clockwise from above: The American Bell P-39 Airacobra. (US National Archives, College Park, Maryland, Still Pictures Branch); The American XP-51 Mustang. (NASA Langley Research Center); The British Supermarine Spitfire Mk5a. (NASA Langley Research Center).

The Italian Macchi C205 Veltro ('Greyhound'). The Veltro suffered from the same deficiencies that plagued the Folgore and could also have caused serious problems for the Allies. (US National Archives, College Park, Maryland, Still Pictures Branch)

The Italian Macchi C202 Folgore ('Thunderbolt') was lightly armed and had it been more heavily armed and produced in greater numbers, it would have undoubtedly hindered Allied victory in the Southern European, Mediterranean and Middle Eastern theatres of action. This particular aircraft was evaluated by the USAAF at Wright Field following the Second World War, restored and is now on static display in the United States as part of the National Air & Space Museum's (Smithsonian Institution) World War II Fighters Gallery in Washington DC. (US National Archives, College Park, Maryland, Still Pictures Branch)

3

THE BIRTH OF AN AERIAL LEGEND:

BUILDING AND TEST FLYING THE FIRST SPITFIRE

R.J. MITCHELL'S CONCEPTION OF THE SPITFIRE DESIGN

Without doubt, R.J. Mitchell's crowning achievement was his conception of the Supermarine Spitfire design. Mitchell used his S5 and S6 series seaplane racers as the base designs to which he added further modifications and refinements to produce one of the world's ultimate air superiority fighters, the Supermarine Spitfire Mk1. In 1934, Mitchell began developing a new advanced fighter that featured retractable landing gear, a closed canopy and thin wings, and became known as the Type 300 pursuit aircraft. In 1935, an improved version of the Type 300 that also featured a more powerful Rolls-Royce Merlin engine was designated the F10/35 and approved for production by the British Air Ministry. This aircraft became the Supermarine Spitfire Mk1 prototype (K5054).

Before the Spitfire rolled off the assembly line at Supermarine Aviation Works Ltd, Southampton, the German Messerschmitt Me 109 had already been produced. The Me 109, designed by Willy Messerschmitt and Robert Lusser, was the product of the National Socialist (Nazi) quest to rearm Germany for world domination, and the Me 109, produced in violation of the terms of the Versailles Treaty, was intended by the Germans to serve as their air superiority fighter.

In 1937, Germany's Me 109 captured the world speed record for aircraft. Me 109s and Spitfires would later clash in an epic battle for aerial supremacy that became known as the Battle of Britain during the Second World War. Although the Me 109 held all of the speed records heading into the Second

A German Messerschmitt Me 109 prototype in flight. The Me 109 captured the world air speed record for Germany in 1937. (US National Archives, College Park, Maryland, Still Pictures Branch)

World War, R.J. Mitchell and the Supermarine team truly believed that the Spitfire was faster, and during the Second World War, later and more advanced versions of the Spitfire reached speeds in high-altitude dives that approached the sound barrier.

A Messerschmitt Me 109 prototype parked on an airfield in Germany in 1937. The Me 109 and the Spitfire served as the primary dogfighters during the Battle of Britain. (US National Archives, College Park, Maryland, Still Pictures Branch)

OVERVIEW OF SPITFIRE PRODUCTION FACILITIES

In June 1936, the Air Ministry requested the production of 310 Spitfires. Spitfires were initially produced at the original Supermarine Works plant in Woolston, Southampton. However, production problems arose and Supermarine was unable to meet the Air Ministry's initial order of 310 aircraft. The company's limited size and emphasis on the production of flying boats hindered Spitfire production. Simultaneously, Vickers was overburdened with Wellington bomber production.

To augment production of Spitfires at Supermarine's aircraft production plant at Southampton, the Air Ministry purchased land for a 'shadow factory' in July 1938, adjacent to the Castle Bromwich Aerodrome in Birmingham. Modernised manufacturing machinery was quickly put into place, but this new factory experienced manufacturing technique, work force management and labour difficulties. Consequently, the plant was turned over to Vickers-Armstrong, which responded by producing ten Spitfire Mk2s by June 1940 and a total of 116 additional Mk2s by September 1940.[12]

Approximately 12,129 Spitfires of various marks had been produced at Castle Bromwich when Spitfire production ceased there in June 1945. The Castle Bromwich Aircraft Factory (CBAF) was the largest producer of Spitfires during the Second World War.

EARLY SPITFIRE MK1 PROTOTYPE FLIGHT TEST RESULTS AND A DESCRIPTION OF THE AIRCRAFT'S REMARKABLE DESIGN

The Supermarine Spitfire Mk1 prototype (K5054) was flown for the first time by Vickers chief test pilot Captain Joseph 'Mutt' Summers, at Eastleigh Aerodrome on 5 March 1936. Jeffrey Quill and George Pickering later took over Spitfire flight-testing duties. Early flight test reports were favourable with the aircraft attaining a top speed of 330mph.

The advanced technological achievement embodied in the Spitfire's design, as well as the status of Supermarine Aviation Works Ltd at Southampton in June–July 1936 was once again described by the NACA's technical assistant in Europe, John J. Ide, in a report entitled 'Visit to England, June–July 1936' and sent back to NACA Headquarters in Washington DC:

> About 1700 men are now employed at the Supermarine Aviation factory which is being much enlarged despite its cramped position on the water front.
>
> 'Spitfire I' (figs. 38–42) – The 'Spitfire I' (1000hp Rolls-Royce Merlin) is claimed to be the fastest military airplane in the world, having a speed of 325–330 miles per hour at 15,000 feet. Its landing speed (with split flaps) is nearly 70 miles per hour. The Air Ministry has ordered 300 examples of this airplane which is completely metallic, including the wing covering. The wing,

elliptical in plan, has a single spar. The wing section based upon NACA 0024, has a progressive washout. Whereas the upper surface of the wing is stressed, the lower plating contributes little to the strength, having openings for the landing wheels and the ammunition boxes of the 8 browning machine guns.

The ducted radiator, instead of being below the fuselage, is under the right wing root, the oil radiator being similarly placed on the left. As this enables the fuselage to be shallower than with the normal arrangement, the additional piping is considered justified.

A special feature is the Alclad fuel tank integral with the fuselage, smooth external surface being obtained by De Bergh countersunk riveting. It is claimed that the whole structure weight has been brought down to a point not hitherto reached in the fighter class.

The following characteristics of the 'Spitfire I' were obtained:

Span	36ft 10in
Length	29ft 11in
Area (including fuselage bottom)	242sq.ft
Area (wings only)	220sq.ft
Aileron area	18.9sq.ft
Total weight	5,100lbs[13]

Ide also noted in his report that the Supermarine 'Spitfire I' (K5054) was displayed at the Royal Air Force display at Hendon on 27 June.[14]

Further flight testing of the Spitfire Mk1 prototype (K5054) revealed the aerodynamic soundness of the aircraft's design and the relative ease with which it could be flown. These factors undoubtedly made training new pilots for Spitfire operations easier. As stated in the official *Handling Trials of the Spitfire K.5054* report (these tests were conducted at the Aeroplane and Armament Experimental Establishment at Martlesham Heath in September 1936):

The aeroplane is simple and easy to fly and has no vices. All controls are entirely satisfactory for this type and no modification to them is required, except that the elevator control might be improved by reducing the gear ratio between the control column and elevator. The controls are well harmonised and appear to give an excellent compromise between manoeuvrability and steadiness for shooting. Take-off and landing are straightforward and easy.

The aeroplane has rather a flat glide, even when the undercarriage and flaps are down and has a considerable float if the approach is made a little too fast. This defect could be remedied by fitting higher drag flaps.

Side view of the Spitfire Mk1 prototype (K5054) in March 1936. (US National Archives, College Park, Maryland, Still Pictures Branch)

A close-up view of the radiator and landing gear of a Spitfire Mk1 prototype. (US National Archives, College Park, Maryland, Still Pictures Branch)

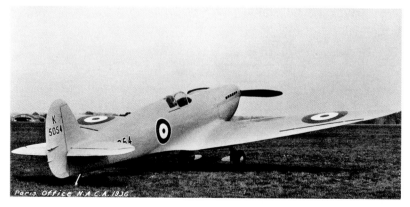

A rear view of the Spitfire Mk1 prototype (K5054). (US National Archives, College Park, Maryland, Still Pictures Branch)

In general the handling of this aeroplane is such that it can be flown by the average fully trained service fighter pilot, but there can be no doubt that it would be improved by having flaps giving a higher drag.[15]

Following the untimely passing of R.J. Mitchell in June 1937, Joseph Smith assumed oversight of further Spitfire design, development and production. Smith served as an excellent successor to Mitchell and, along with his faithful Supermarine team, designed and developed the numerous Spitfire marks (versions) that followed the Mk1. When the NACA's John J. Ide returned to England to visit and survey the status of aeronautics progress at various government, military and industrial facilities and bases throughout the country in July 1938, he made special note of the problems hindering further Spitfire development and production efforts:

There has been an extremely long delay in getting the Spitfire fighter into production. A major difficulty was the fact that while the main wing spar and nose section of the wing are built by Supermarine, the rear portion of the wing has been built under subcontract by General Aircraft (the firm which produced the Monospar airplane) which had no experience in the field of metal construction. The tail units are supplied by Folland Aircraft at Hamble and have been quite satisfactory. The fuselages are built by Supermarine, and final assembly of the whole airplane takes place at the Eastleigh airport outside of Southampton.

Of the production order for 500 Spitfires received by the Supermarine Company, only the first three examples had been flown up to the time of my visit. From now on, however, the production should be encountering no major difficulties.

The factory is sending 5 airplanes to Martlesham Heath to be flown 500 hours each in the least possible time. Lord Nuffield wisely refuses to start his order of 1,000 Spitfires in the factory building at Castle Bromwich until the possibility of numerous changes is eliminated.

Over 100 fuselages have been built in the 16 jigs at the factory and are stored at Eastleigh awaiting completion of the wings. The rear of the fuselage is a true monocoque structure but the forward portion is a semimonocoque [sic].

A direct rear view of the Spitfire Mk1 prototype (K5054). (US National Archives, College Park, Maryland, Still Pictures Branch)

The Spitfire Mk1 prototype (K5054) in flight. (US National Archives, College Park, Maryland, Still Pictures Branch)

The main spar has a section shown in the sketch. The web is solid. Each flange at the wing root is built up of a nest of five square tubes with rounded corners, the tubes stopping at various points toward the tips as the stresses are reduced. The skin over the leading edge of the wing forward of the spar is about ¹⁄₁₀ inch thick, whereas the rear skin is only ¹⁄₂₅ of an inch thick. The wing structure behind the spar is decidedly meager [*sic*], large gaps being required by the wheels, 8 guns and landing lights. Split flaps are fitted to the wings inboard of the ailerons.

To determine the drag of protruding rivets under actual flight conditions, a multitude of split peas were placed over the rivets being glued with seccotine. This material was used as it is easily removable with water, unlike casein glue. Quick progressive removal was necessary as the experiments had to be completed in one day to avoid the effect of changes in the atmosphere.

From the tests it appeared that if all rivets were projecting the maximum speed was reduced by 20mph. The production model of the Spitfire has countersunk rivets over the entire wing but protruding heads along several horizontal rows on the fuselage surface, these apparently having a negligible effect on performance.

The Rolls Royce Merlin II engine, having a maximum rpm of 3,000 with +6-¼ pound boost, is prestone-cooled and has in the nose a semicircular [*sic*] header tank. It was stated that in the near future this medium will be abandoned and replaced by water in connection with 'pressure cooling,' in which the pressure of 10 pounds is maintained in the radiator, giving a high boiling point and small radiator size.

The low-velocity radiator of the Spitfire is fitted in the left wing root. Half of the radiator projects into the wing and half is below the bottom surface. The air exits through a slot the size of which is controlled by a flap. The oil cooler is under the right wing.

A Vickers retractable oleo landing gear with a single strut is used. The hand pump requires 20 seconds to raise the wheels into the wing recesses. The tail wheel is not retractable.

The engine is fitted with new Rolls Royce ejector exhaust manifold. Thus equipped the Spitfire has a maximum speed of 356mph at 12,000 feet.

Although a wooden two-blade propeller is fitted, provision has been made for a controllable-pitch propeller. Hence ballast is placed on either side of the engine with the present propeller.

The first 12 production airplanes are arranged to take antispinning [*sic*] parachutes housed in the top fairing of the fuselage. To avoid fouling, there is a guard over the rudder.

The cockpit is quite roomy but for a tall pilot using a seat parachute, there is not much headroom under the sliding cockpit cover. One thumb button on the control stick fires the 8 Browning guns mechanically. A buzzer sounds if the throttle is closed while the wheels are retracted.

Of the two tanks in the fuselage, one holds 59 and the other 44 and ½ US gallons. The supply is deemed adequate for two hours' cruising at 280mph.

Tests are being made with compressed wood impregnated with synthetic resin according to the Jablo process for the construction of rib flanges into which the skin would be screwed.

The Supermarine Company has nearly completed the racing version of the Spitfire built to attack the speed record now held by Germany. A special Merlin engine developing over 2,000 horsepower and using pressure cooling will be used. The wings have been cut down by removing the detachable tips of the normal Spitfire and rounding off the ends.

Among the experimental airplanes under way, is a single-seat fighter with two Merlin engines to compete with the Westland and the four-engine bomber built to specification B 12/36 reported last year.

The factory continues to build Walrus amphibians at the rate of five per week. I saw the first example of the Walrus replacement. The new airplane has a Perseus tractor instead of a Pegasus pusher, and the engine has been raised to the upper wing instead of being placed nearly midway between the wings. The new type in addition to being stressed for catapulting, is adapted for deck landing, which the Walrus is not.

Production continues on the Stranraer biplane flying boat (2 Pegasus X engines). Assembly of this flying boat is done at Hythe.[16]

The Spitfire racer, dubbed the 'Speed Spitfire' (Type 323), that Ide referred to in his report was completed soon after his visit to England and wore a royal blue and silver paint scheme. Just a few months prior to this aircraft's completion, the Germans established yet another world air speed record of 394.6mph with Hitler's propaganda fighter, the Heinkel He 100 V2. The Speed Spitfire, flown for the first time on 11 November 1938, surpassed this air speed on another test flight in February 1939, attaining a top speed of 408mph at 3,000ft.

Unfortunately for Britain, Germany once again pushed the limits of high-speed flight further when its Heinkel He 100 V8 attained a top speed of 463.9mph on 30 March 1939 and its Messerschmitt Me 209 V1 attained a top

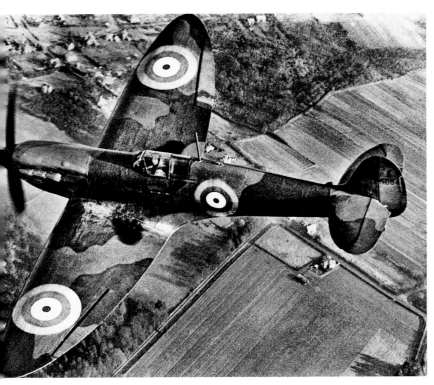

The Spitfire Mk1 prototype (K5054) wearing camouflage in flight in 1938. (US National Archives, College Park, Maryland, Textual Reference Branch)

Aeroplane and Armament Experimental Establishment
Martlesham Heath
6 January 1939
Spitfire K.9787
Merlin II
Fixed pitch wooden airscrew
Performance Trials

Results of Trials

A comparison is made in the table below between this production aeroplane and the prototype K.5054.

	Prototype K.5054	Production K.9787
Maximum speed	349 at 16,800ft	362 at 18,500ft
Maximum cruising speed (at 15,000ft)	311mph	318mph
Time to 15,000ft	5.7mins	6.5mins
Time to 30,000ft	17mins	22.4mins
Service ceiling	35,400ft	31,900ft
Weight	5332lb	5819lb[17]

speed of 469.22mph on 26 April 1939, in both instances setting new world air speed records. It became evident that the Speed Spitfire had to undergo significant improvements and refinements to catch up with the Germans.

Britain, however, turned its attention from battling Germany in the conquest of the world's air speed record to battling Germany in a life or death struggle in the skies during a time of world war. Consequently, efforts to capture the world air speed record were abandoned, and the Speed Spitfire was converted to a photo reconnaissance (PR) Mk2 aircraft.

The first production Spitfires entered operational service with 19 Squadron in August 1938. On 6 January 1939, flight trials and comparisons were made between the prototype Spitfire Mk1 (K5054) and the first production Spitfire Mk1 (K9787) at the Aeroplane and Armament Experimental Establishment at Martlesham Heath. The results were quite revealing and are disclosed in the following table:

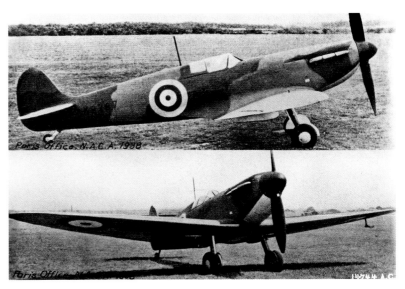

The first production Spitfire Mk1 (K9787) in 1938. (US National Archives, College Park, Maryland, Still Pictures Branch)

The ninth production Spitfire Mk1 (K9795) of 19 Squadron in flight, in 1938.
(Royal Air Force)

Opposite: K9787 in flight over the British coast in May 1938. (US National Archives,
College Park, Maryland, Still Pictures Branch)

Some of the first production Spitfire Mk1s operational with 19 Squadron in formation, in
1938. (Royal Air Force)

HOW THE SPITFIRE MK1 MATCHED UP AGAINST THE OPPOSITION

Two months before the start of one of history's greatest air battles, the Battle of Britain, British war planners and Supermarine officials had the opportunity to evaluate the Spitfire's strengths and weaknesses when going up against its primary dogfighting adversary in the coming epic struggle, the German Messerschmitt Me 109. A Me 109 E-3 fell into British hands intact and participated in a fly-off with a Spitfire Mk1 in June 1940. The results of this fly-off were as follows:

Royal Aircraft Establishment at Farnborough

June 1940

Spitfire IA K.9791 with Rotol constant speed propeller

Me.109E-3 Werk-Nr 1304

Comparative trials between the Me.109 and 'Rotol' Spitfire.

1. The trial commenced with the two aircraft taking off together, with the Spitfire slightly behind and using +6¼lb boost and 3,000rpm.

2. When fully airborne, the pilot of the Spitfire reduced his revolutions to 2,650rpm and was then able to overtake and out climb the Me 109. At 4,000ft, the Spitfire pilot was 1,000 feet above the Me 109, from which position he was able to get on its tail, and remain there within effective range despite all efforts of the pilot of the Me 109 to shake him off.

3. The Spitfire then allowed the Me 109 to get on to his tail and attempted to shake him off this he found quite easy owing to the superior manoeuvrability of his aircraft, particularly in the looping plane and at low speeds between 100 and 140 mph. By executing a steep turn just above stalling speed, he ultimately got back into a position on the tail of the Me 109.

4. Another effective form of evasion with the Spitfire was found to be a steep, climbing spiral at 120mph, using +6¼ boost and 2,650rpm; in this manoeuvre, the Spitfire gained rapidly on the Me 109, eventually allowing the pilot to execute a half roll, on to the tail of his opponent.

5. Comparative speed trials were then carried out, and the Spitfire proved to be considerably the faster of the two, both in acceleration and straight and level flight, without having to make use of the emergency +12 boost. During diving trials, the Spitfire pilot found that, by engaging fully coarse pitch and using −2lbs boost, his aircraft was superior to the Me 109.[18]

In June 1940, a captured German Me 109E-3 was test flown in simulated combat against Spitfire Mk1a K9791 at the Royal Aircraft Establishment at Farnborough, England. (US National Archives, College Park, Maryland, Still Pictures Branch)

As revealed in these trial results, the Spitfire possessed virtually no weaknesses in simulated aerial combat with its Me 109 adversary. These results would help convince British war planners that the Spitfire should be used for dogfighting German fighter escorts and the Hawker Hurricane for bomber busting during the Battle of Britain.

A TRUE ANGLO-AMERICAN DEVELOPMENT EFFORT AND TESTIMONY FROM A SPITFIRE TEST PILOT

The development of the fighter and photo-reconnaissance variants of the Supermarine Spitfire was, however, truly an Anglo-American effort. In the United States in 1922, revolutionary research that would have a profound effect on aeronautics progress worldwide was initiated in a unique new wind tunnel at the NACA's Langley Memorial Aeronautical Laboratory (LMAL) in Hampton, Virginia. The wind tunnel, essentially a steel pressure cylinder constructed at the Newport News Shipyard in Virginia, became known as the Variable Density Tunnel (VDT) and was designed to develop and study advanced low-drag aerofoils at high Reynolds numbers.

The VDT was designed by a group of researchers led by Max M. Munk, who had earlier emigrated from Göttingen, Germany, to the United States and NACA Langley. Munk was a brilliant pupil of the renowned German professor, Ludwig Prandtl. Under the direction of Munk, American researchers, Ira H. Abbott and Albert Von Doenhoff, helped develop what became known as the 'bible', or detailed comprehensive catalogue of low-drag aerofoils that were incorporated on aircraft designs of both allied and axis countries immediately prior to and during the Second World War (from the late 1930s to 1945).

Later, during the late 1930s and 1940s, the famous laminar flow airfoil that helped make the North American P-51 Mustang such an effective piston-engined air superiority fighter during the Second World War was developed and perfected in the NACA Langley Low Turbulence Pressure Tunnel (LTPT) by researcher Eastman N. Jacobs, as well as other NACA advanced aerofoils that were used by European countries on advanced jet fighter designs.

Among the aerofoils developed by the American researchers at NACA Langley during the 1930s was a series of NACA low-drag aerodynamic aerofoils incorporated in the wing designs of all marks of the Supermarine Spitfire and Seafire – the low-drag NACA 2213 series aerofoil.[19]

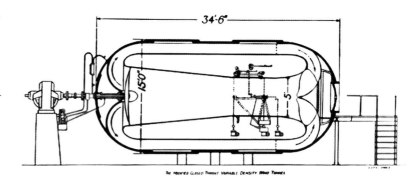

1928 VDT Operations Schematic. (NASA Langley Research Center)

Engineers at NACA Langley operating the VDT in 1929. (NASA Langley Research Center)

Max Munk poses beside the VDT in 1922. (NASA Langley Research Center)

Eastman N. Jacobs. (NASA Langley Research Center)

A view from the air of the Low Turbulence Pressure Tunnel (LTPT) at NACA Langley in April 1940. (NASA Langley Research Center)

LTPT construction in 1940. (NASA Langley Research Center)

An aircraft flap edge being tested in the LTPT in 1998. (NASA Langley Research Center)

Beginning in late 1943, British Royal Navy Seafires performed carrier suitability trials by making arrested landings on this turntable carrier-deck landing platform simulator at Naval Air Station Patuxent River, Maryland, US. (US National Archives, College Park, Maryland, Still Pictures Branch)

In addition, important developmental flight and carrier suitability tests on various Spitfire and Seafire marks were conducted at NACA Langley; the United States Army Air Force's (USAAF) Wright Field (now Wright-Patterson AFB) in Dayton, Ohio; and the United States Navy's Naval Air Station Patuxent River (Pax River) in southern Maryland.

Following Britain's entry into the Second World War, Vickers Supermarine charged Jeffrey Quill with the task of serving as the company's chief test pilot. He also managed a team of twelve test pilots who, together with Quill, test flew all of the prototype Spitfires of all marks (versions) produced during the Second World War. Castle Bromwich's chief test pilot, Alex Henshaw, also participated in the flight testing of some of the Spitfire prototypes. He later elaborated on his test flight experiences with the Spitfire stating:

I loved the Spitfire in all of her many versions. But I have to admit that the later marks, although they were faster than the earlier ones, were also much heavier and so did not handle so well. You did not have such positive control over them. One test of manoeuvrability was to throw her into a flick-roll and see how many times she rolled. With the Mark II or the Mark V one got two-and-a-half flick-rolls but the Mark IX was heavier and you got only one-and-a-half. With the later and still heavier versions, one got even less. The essence of aircraft design is compromise, and an improvement at one end of the performance envelope is rarely achieved without a deterioration somewhere else.[20, 21]

4

BUILDING SPITFIRES FOR WAR

FIGHTER/FIGHTER-BOMBER SPITFIRE VARIANTS

Production, Flight Testing and Development of the Spitfire Mk2

The Supermarine Spitfire Mk2 was an advanced version of the Mk1, featuring a more powerful Merlin 12 engine. The Mk2 received the most attention in production efforts at the CBAF and was the most numerously produced Spitfire there.

The Mk2s also featured Rotol wide-bladed propellers. The addition of a more powerful engine and advanced propeller made the Mk2 faster than the Mk1. However, a significant weight gain made the aircraft slower than some of the first Spitfires produced. By April 1941, Mk2s were in widespread use with RAF units and became the exclusive Spitfire used in combat at the time. Always seeking to extend the range of the Spitfire to help escort heavy bombers, British war planners and Supermarine pursued the development of 'long range' Spitfires in 1941. As a result, some Mk2s were equipped with fixed 40 gallon fuel tanks, located beneath their starboard wings.

The Spitfire Mk2a featured the normal eight-machine-gun armament configuration, but the Mk2b featured two cannon and four machine guns in the wings. In his excellent book, *Famous Fighters of the Second World War* (volume one, 1965), William Green described the impact that cannon-armed Spitfires had on air battles over Europe, as well as the evolution of the Mk2 into the Mk5:

Some cannon-armed Spitfires were operational during the 'Battle of Britain' in 1940, and the first operational success with a cannon-armed Spitfire was recorded as early as March 1940, although the cannon armament was looked upon with mixed feelings by Spitfire pilots, for the gun was not without its share of teething troubles. Of the 920 Spitfire IIs built, 170 were completed as Mark IIBs with cannon armament, and a number of older Spitfire Is were converted to Mark IB standard. The next step was to produce a universal wing (the 'C' wing, Type 346) which could take either two Hispano cannon, one cannon and two machine guns, or four machine guns. This was first introduced on the Mark VC which differed from the Mark VA and VB in having a strengthened undercarriage with the wheels moved two inches forward, and a further increase in armour from 129lb on the Mark VA and 152lb on the VB, to 193lb.[22]

Early flight trials of the first Spitfire Mk2 produced (P7280), conducted at the Aeroplane and Armament Experimental Establishment at Boscombe Down, England, in May 1940, were documented in the following flight-test report:

In accordance with Air Ministry letter, dated 30th May, 1940, short performance and handling tests have been carried out on this aeroplane, the first Nuffield-built Spitfire II, to compare it with the standard Spitfire I.

Opposite: A Spitfire assembly line in the cavernous Castle Bromwich Aircraft Factory during the Second World War. (Vickers Archives/Syndics Cambridge University Library)

1.0 Comments on Trials

This aeroplane was fitted with a bullet-proof windscreen, armour plating over the petrol tank and externally, apart from the radiator, was similar to the Rotol Spitfire I, N.3171, previously tested at this establishment. The radiator of P.7280 is of the Morris type and tests were called for to determine the suitability of this radiator under tropical conditions. Internally, one difference between this aeroplane and N.3171 has been the fitting of armour plating behind the pilot in the Spitfire II. Generally, any change in performance or handling can be attributed to the change in engine and radiator alone.

Conclusions

The handling and flying characteristics are practically unaltered by the change in engine though there is a slight decrease in stability on the climb. Below full throttle height the improvement in performance of the aeroplane is less than expected when the extra power of the Merlin XII engine is taken into consideration. This matter is being investigated by Messrs. Rolls-Royse [sic], Limited. Above rated height the improvement in climb is satisfactory, as is the increase in the ceiling of the aeroplane. The cooling system is inadequate for summer conditions.

Miscellaneous

Deliveries of Spitfire IIs began in June 1940. No. 611 fully converted to Spitfire IIs in August 1940, thus being the first squadron to become fully operational with the type. Nos. 266 and 74 followed in early September, with Nos. 19 and 66 switching during the latter half of the month. In October, it was 41 and 603 squadrons turn, bringing to 7 the number of squadrons to fully equip with this variant during the Battle of Britain.[23]

Production, Flight Testing and Development of the Spitfire Mk3

Efforts to continually modernise and enhance the base Spitfire concept culminated in the development of the Mk3. Late mark Spitfire design characteristics were featured in the Mk3 design, including incorporation of the Merlin 20 engine power plant. The Mk3 also featured a shortened wingspan of 30ft 6in and a stretching of the fuselage to 30ft 4in. The Mk3 also possessed sturdier landing gear that was positioned more forward than on previous Spitfire designs for improved stability upon taxiing, take-off and landing. Unlike previous Spitfire marks, the Mk3 also had wheel covers to keep the wheels protected upon retraction of the landing gear. The Mk3 also possessed a tailwheel that could be retracted into a recess within the rear fuselage.

Other design advancements found in the Mk3 included a bulletproof windscreen. Spitfire Mk3 N3297 was the first Mk3 to be produced and flew for the first time on 16 March 1940. The following year, Spitfire Mk5 W3237 was modified into a Mk3 and served as a test subject well into the latter years of the Second World War.

Despite favourable flight test results, British war planners decided to reserve the small number of Merlin 20 engine power plants for Hawker Hurricane 2 fighters. As a result, the Spitfire Mk3 faded into obscurity. However, Spitfire Mk3 N3297 (redesignated Type 348) was later re-equipped with a more powerful Merlin engine and served as the Spitfire Mk9 prototype.

Production, Flight Testing and Development of the Spitfire Mk5

In 1941, Germany began conducting high-altitude photo reconnaissance overflights of England using Junkers Ju 86Ps equipped with pressurised cockpits and cabins. Weary of and annoyed by this new aerial threat, British war planners requested the production of a high-altitude, pressurised Spitfire to be equipped with a yet more powerful Merlin engine. However, production efforts took longer than expected and British war planners and Supermarine decided to pursue development of the Supermarine Spitfire Mk5.

For the Spitfire Mk5 design, a Spitfire Mk1, using a Merlin 45 engine, was used as the base design initially. The engine was revolutionary due to the fact that it utilised a supercharger. Mk2 Spitfires were also converted into Mk5s.

Air Fighting Development Unit Spitfire Mk2as flying over Duxford, England, on 6 April 1942. (Royal Air Force)

A German Junkers Ju 86P high-altitude photo reconnaissance aircraft. (Royal Air Force)

Mk5s became operational with several RAF fighter squadrons in early 1941. In fly-offs with a captured German Messerschmitt Me 109F, the Spitfire Mk5 was faster than the Me 109F and possessed a better climb rate.[24] The CBAF undertook the production of most of the Mk5s during the Second World War. A total of three major Mk5 variants were manufactured during the war.

The Supermarine Spitfire Mk5a

The Supermarine Spitfire Mk5a possessed the same wing design and armament configuration (eight Browning machine guns in the wings) as the Spitfire Mk2. Ninety-four Spitfire Mk5as were produced during the Second World War. Two Mk5as, R7347 and W3119, served as special developmental testbeds and were extensively test flown by the USAAF at Wright Field, Dayton, Ohio, and the NACA at the Langley Memorial Aeronautical Laboratory (LMAL) in Hampton, Virginia, USA. The NACA flight tests included flight studies to determine the flying qualities and stalling characteristics of the Spitfire as well as flight studies of a new 'jet' exhaust system. It was a Mk5a that received the dubious distinction, however, of being the aircraft that the famous British RAF ace Douglas Bader was shot down in over France on 9 August 1941. Bader was captured by the Germans and served out the remainder of the war in a POW camp.

Performance trials for the Spitfire Mk5a were performed by Spitfire Mk5a X4922 at the Aeroplane and Armament Experimental Establishment at Boscombe Down, England, on 29 April 1941. The results were as follows:

(a) The top speed of the aeroplane is 375mph at 20,800 feet.
(b) The maximum rate of climb is 3,140 feet per minute at 14,400 feet. The time to 20,000 feet is 7.1 minutes and the Service ceiling is 37,700 feet.
(c) The radiator is not quite suitable for English summer conditions on the climb.
(d) The oil cooler is suitable for English summer conditions on the climb.
(e) The take-off run in zero wind and standard conditions is 330 yards, and the distance to clear a 50 foot screen is 530 yards.
(f) The airscrew setting of 34 deg. to 54 deg. is suitable for the aeroplane under all conditions of flight.[25]

Flying qualities investigation flight testing of a Mk5a at NACA Langley solidified the point to Americans that the Spitfire was a superb fighter aircraft. As stated in the 'Conclusions' section of the flight-test report:

Two Second World War game changers (an RAF P-51 Mustang and RAF Spitfire Mk5a) and an RAF Bomber Command Vickers Wellington medium bomber return to their base following a tactical exercise on 29 June 1943. The Mustang and Spitfire performed simulated interception attacks on the Wellington, which was supposed to represent a German bomber invading British airspace. (The New York Times/Redux, US National Archives, College Park, Maryland, Still Pictures Branch)

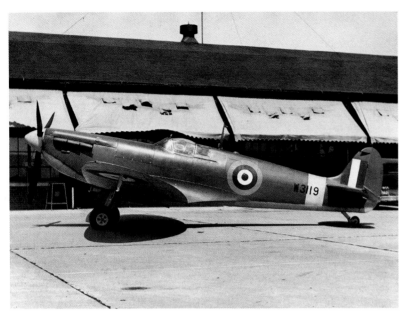

A developmental/test Spitfire Mk5a (W3119) on the tarmac at Wright Field on 29 July 1941. (US National Archives, College Park, Maryland, Still Pictures Branch)

Another developmental/test Spitfire Mk5a (R7347) on the flying field at Wright Field on 2 September 1941. (US National Archives, College Park, Maryland, Still Pictures Branch)

Spitfire Mk5a (W3119) in flight over Wright Field on 29 July 1941. (US National Archives, College Park, Maryland, Still Pictures Branch)

R7347 on the flying field at Wright Field on 2 September 1941. (US National Archives, College Park, Maryland, Still Pictures Branch)

R7347 in flight over Wright Field on 6 April 1943. (US National Archives, College Park, Maryland, Still Pictures Branch)

The flying qualities of the Supermarine Spitfire airplane observed in these tests may be summarised in terms of the accepted standards for satisfactory flying qualities as follows:

1   The short-period longitudinal oscillation was satisfactorily heavily damped in all conditions tested.

2   In all flight conditions the stick-fixed longitudinal stability was either neutral or unstable, and therefore failed to meet the accepted requirements. The requirement for a stable stick-force gradient was met in all conditions of flight except for the condition with flaps down, power on.

3   The stick-force gradient in maneuvers was 5.0 pounds per g. The requirement for a force gradient of less than 6 pounds per g was therefore satisfied.

4   The stick motion required to stall in maneuvers was ¾ inch. This value is much less than the 4-inch stick travel recommended for satisfactory flying qualities.

5   The elevator control was adequate for landing and take-off.

6   The longitudinal trim changes due to changes in engine power, flap position, or landing-gear position were exceptionally small.

7   The power of the elevator trim tabs was adequate.

8   The damping of the control-free lateral oscillation was satisfactory. No undesirable short-period lateral oscillations were noted.

9   The aileron control was adequate at low speeds but unsatisfactory at high speeds because of the excessive stick forces required to obtain high rolling velocities.

10   Aileron yaw was within the limits specified as acceptable.

11   The dihedral effect was stable except in left sideslips with power on, where it was practically neutral.

12   The rudder was sufficiently powerful to offset aileron yaw and to maintain directional control during landing and take-off. The rudder forces required were well below the upper limit of 180 pounds specified.

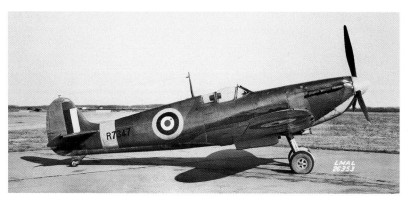

Spitfire Mk5a (R7347) at the NACA Langley Memorial Aeronautical Laboratory, in Hampton, Virginia, in September 1942. (US National Archives, College Park, Maryland, Still Pictures Branch)

Rear view of R7347 at the NACA Langley Memorial Aeronautical Laboratory in September 1942. (US National Archives, College Park, Maryland, Still Pictures Branch)

Front view of R7347 at the NACA Langley Memorial Aeronautical Laboratory in September 1942. (US National Archives, College Park, Maryland, Still Pictures Branch)

13   Directional stability was satisfactory.

14   A large pitching moment due to sideslip existed.

15   The stalling characteristics in normal flight or in maneuvers [sic] were excellent though the maximum lift coefficients were low. No understandable ground-looping tendencies were noted.[26]

The Supermarine Spitfire Mk5b

The Mk5b was the most numerously produced Spitfire of the Mk5 series. The Mk5b made use of a more powerful Merlin 45 engine and the new B wing, capable of accommodating eight .303 Browning machine guns, a combination of four .303 Browning machine guns and two 20mm cannon, or four 20mm cannon. The Mk5b possessed features that were commonly found on the Spitfire variants to follow. Initially, Supermarine modified a few Mk1s, making them into the first Mk5bs. The conventional exhaust stacks found on earlier versions of the Spitfire were modified into 'fishtail' exhaust stacks. This modification led to a performance enhancement.

Beginning with the development of the Mk5b in 1941, alloy ailerons were now a common feature on Spitfires.[27] Malcolm Hood canopies, designed for enhanced pilot comfort and vision, also became the norm in Spitfire marks, starting with the Mk5b. To increase the range of the Mk5b, the 'slipper' drop tank was developed and was carried in a fixed position on the underside of the aircraft along the fuselage/wings mid-section.

In August 1941, a new German fighter threat was encountered over the English Channel that challenged British air superiority. This threat emerged in the form of the excellent Focke-Wulf Fw 190A-3 'Butcher Bird'. To combat this threat, some Mk5bs had clipped wings for improved manoeuvrability and speed at low altitudes. However, despite this performance improvement, the British Mk5s suffered terrible losses against the Fw 190s and it quickly became clear that a new, more advanced Spitfire would be needed to wrestle air superiority back from the Germans. This would later appear in the form of the Mk9.

A tropicalised version of the Spitfire, designated the Mk5b Trop, was developed for air combat in North Africa and the Middle East, and also for aerial combat in the Pacific. The Mk5b Trop was outfitted with a huge Vokes air filter on the underside of the aircraft's nose for operation in dusty and

The German Focke-Wulf Fw 190A-3 'Butcher Bird' that was mistakenly landed by its pilot on a British airfield on 14 May 1943. The aircraft was lost in fog over the English Channel and the pilot mistook the British airfield for a German airfield in France. (US National Archives, College Park, Maryland, Still Pictures Branch)

Front view of the Focke-Wulf Fw 190A-3 previously shown. (US National Archives, College Park, Maryland, Still Pictures Branch)

sandy environments. It was soon found, however, that the oversized filter degraded the aircraft's performance, but only slightly.

On 18 June 1941, Spitfire Mk5b performance trials were conducted at the Aeroplane and Armament Experimental Establishment in Boscombe Down, England, using Spitfire Mk5b W3134. The trials were described in a flight test report as follows:

1. Introduction.

Brief performance trials were required of a Spitfire Mk VB fully operationally equipped for comparison with two other aircraft of the type not operationally equipped and previously tested at this establishment. The suffix 'B' after the type denotes that the aeroplane is fitted with 2-20mm. guns and four 0.303 inch guns. A standard Spitfire I airscrew was fitted with the blade settings at 54 degrees coarse and 34 degrees fine.

The weight of the plane was 6525lb and the centre of gravity was at 7.8 inches aft of the datum.

It was also desired to find the effect on performance of fitting a snowguard to the air-intake.

2. Results of tests.

(a) The top speed of the aeroplane is 371mph at 20,100 feet.

(b) With the snowguard fitted the top speed falls to 365mph at 18,800 feet.

(c) The maximum rate of climb is 3,250 feet per minute at 15,200ft

(d) The time to 20,000 feet is 6.4 minutes, and the service ceiling is 37,500 feet.

(e) The effect of the snowguard on the ceiling of the aeroplane is negligible.[28]

When compared to the performance trials of the Spitfire Mk5b Trop, also conducted at the Aeroplane and Armament Experimental Establishment in Boscombe Down on 15 April 1942, it was found that the conventional Mk5b held a distinct speed advantage due, of course, to the addition of the oversized air filter in the nose. A description of the performance trials of the Spitfire Mk5b Trop was provided in a flight test report as follows:

A developmental RAF Spitfire Mk5b in flight. (US National Archives, College Park, Maryland, Still Pictures Branch)

RAF East India Squadron Spitfire Mk5b (underside view) in flight in 1942. (US National Archives, College Park, Maryland, Still Pictures Branch)

A developmental RAF Spitfire Mk5b in flight (front underside view). (US National Archives, College Park, Maryland, Still Pictures Branch)

RAF Spitfire Mk5b peels off. (US National Archives, College Park, Maryland, Still Pictures Branch, Still Pictures Branch)

RAF Spitfire Mk5b comes in for a landing at an RAF airfield on 2 March 1943. (Royal Air Force)

RAF 222 Squadron Spitfire Mk5b in flight in 1942. (Royal Air Force)

Opposite: A developmental RAF Spitfire Mk5b in flight (rear view). (US National Archives, College Park, Maryland)

RAF 303 Polish Squadron Spitfire Mk5b in flight. (Royal Air Force)

An American 71 Eagle Squadron Spitfire Mk5b in 1942. (US Air Force)

SUMMARY

This report deals with performance trials on a fully tropicalised Spitfire V.b. with a Merlin 45 engine, with and without a 90 gallon external fuel tank. The performance results were as follows:

	Without tank	With tank
Weight	6,695lb	7,485lb
Maximum rate of climb	2,660ft/min	2,145ft/min
At full throttle height of	14,000ft	14,000ft
Service ceiling	36,300	34,500ft
Time to 20,000ft	8mins	10mins
Maximum speed	354 mph	337½mph
At full throttle height of	17,400ft	17,400ft [29]

One of the more interesting Spitfire Mk5b developments involved the modification of such an aircraft into a floatplane. The origin and history of this experiment was described in detail by Green (1965):

Another series of experiments concerned the adaptation of the Spitfire as a float seaplane. Such an adaptation was first considered in 1940 in relation to the Norwegian campaign, during which such a floatplane might have been of immense value. A Spitfire I was adapted to take a pair of floats similar to those

A South African Air Force 40 Squadron Spitfire Mk5b Trop at Gabes, Tunisia, in April 1943. The aircraft has clipped wingtips. (Royal Air Force)

fitted to the third Blackburn Roc two-seat naval fighter, but the marriage, which was given the Type 342 designation, had not been consummated by the time the Norwegian campaign had terminated. In 1942 the project was revived, and Supermarine designed a set of floats for the Spitfire VB, having a reserve buoyancy of 90 percent. Made by Folland Aircraft, who also completed the conversion, these floats were attached by cantilever struts to the wing spars some five feet from the aircraft centre line. After successful handline trials with the prototype, the Type 355 (W3760), Folland built twelve sets of these floats, and converted two more Spitfire Vs, one of which was flown for a time in the Mediterranean area.[30]

The Supermarine Spitfire Mk5c

The Supermarine Spitfire Mk5c design incorporated numerous enhancements to the Spitfire design first introduced in the Mk3 and Mk5b, including a sturdier fuselage and landing gear modifications as well as improved windscreen. Type C 'Universal' wings, with bulges on the tops, were incorporated in the Mk5c design. In addition, the Mk5c featured enhanced protection for the pilot in the form of thicker armour.

On 8 March 1942, performance and handling trials were performed in a developmental Spitfire Mk5c (AA873) equipped with four 20mm cannon, at the Aeroplane and Armament Experimental Establishment at Boscombe Down. The results, as revealed in the following report, proved to be favourable:

Summary

1. Introduction.
The advent of the 'universal wing' has made possible three alternative loadings to a Spitfire. When such a wing is fitted the Mark number of the aeroplane is followed by the suffix 'c' and the aeroplane can be flown with 8 – .303" guns, 2 – 20 m/m guns plus 4 – .303" guns, or 4 – 20 m/m guns. Of the three loadings, the first two have been tested and used in previous Spitfires, but the Spitfire at the third loading has not previously been tested for performance and general handling at the A. & A.E.E., and for this reason, brief tests were called for. This report deals with the results of those tests.

2. Condition of aircraft relevant to tests.
Throughout the trials the aircraft was loaded to an all-up weight of 6,917lb with the centre of gravity 7.4" aft of the datum point. The design centre of gravity limits are from 5.0" to 7.7" aft of the datum or from 5.0" to 8.2" aft of the datum including the aft extension.

The aeroplane was fitted with universal wings, 4 - 20 m/m guns and an internal bullet-proof windscreen.

No snow-guard was fitted during the tests.

A rear view mirror was mounted on top of the pilots hood outside, and triple-ejector exhausts were fitted (without fishtails).

I.F.F. aerials, a W/T mast, and aerial were installed.

The aeroplane was fitted with a 7½lb inertia weight in the elevator control circuit.

3. Results of tests

(i) The maximum rate of climb is 2,900 feet/minute at 13,400 feet. The time to 20,000 feet is 7.4 minutes, and the estimated service ceiling is 36,400 feet.

(ii) The top speed is 374mph at 19,000 feet.

(iii) There is no noticeable difference between the handling characteristics of this aeroplane and other Spitfire V types.[31]

USAAF Lt C.C. Porter sits in the cockpit of a British RAF developmental Spitfire Mk5c, equipped with four Hispano 20mm cannon, at Wright Field in Dayton, Ohio, in July 1942. (US National Archives, College Park, Maryland, Still Pictures Branch)

The Mk5c held the distinction of being the first Spitfire to serve as a fighter/bomber, capable of carrying a single 250lb bomb beneath each wing. Other interesting Mk5c developments were noted by Green (1965):

Another Spitfire, a Mark VC, BR372, had split, trailing-edge dive brakes, and AB457 was flown at the Royal Aircraft Establishment with liquid oxygen injection to boost the performance … In the Middle East, in 1942, two Spitfire VCs were modified to undertake an epic series of high-altitude flights, without pressurisation, to combat the high-flying, pressurised Ju 86P and 86R bomber and reconnaissance aircraft. One of these modified Spitfires eventually attained an altitude of nearly 50,000 feet – an incredible performance by both machine and pilot in view of the lack of special high-altitude equipment.[32]

The majority of Mk5cs were used in combat outside of Europe in locales such as North Africa, the Mediterranean and the Far East.

Spitfire Mk5s Slated for Foreign Use and Overall Mk5 Production

Britain's allies greatly benefited from Mk5 production, receiving quite a few Mk5s for their air forces. From 1942–1943, the Royal Australian Air Force (RAAF) received 300 Mk5c Trops, which fought valiantly on several Pacific fronts. From late 1942–1943, the famous American Eagle Squadron was equipped with and flew Mk5bs from airbases in England over Europe. The Soviet Union received 143 Mk5bs.[33] Mk5bs were also provided to Portugal

Royal Canadian Air Force (RCAF) 417 Squadron Spitfire Mk5c Trops prepare to taxi out for take-off at an airfield in Tunisia in 1943. (Royal Air Force)

beginning in 1944 and ending in 1947. The Portuguese Spitfires remained operational until the early 1950s. Egypt and Turkey also received Mk5b Trops.

The final tally regarding the total number of Spitfire Mk5s produced during the Second World War was quite impressive – 94 Mk5as, 3,911 Mk5bs, and 2,467 Mk5cs.[34] The CBAF manufactured the majority of Mk5bs and Mk5cs.

Production, Flight Testing and Development of the Spitfire Mk6

In 1941, Britain and British military bases in the Middle East, specifically Egypt, were being constantly monitored by high-altitude, pressurised cockpit and cabin equipped German Junkers Ju 86P and R bomber/photo-reconnaissance aircraft. To combat this growing threat, the British Air Ministry requested the development of a high-altitude, pressurised cockpit equipped Spitfire interceptor. As stated by Green (1965):

> This called for two principal modifications – the introduction of a pressurised cabin, and the use of an engine suitably rated for higher altitude. The first version of the Spitfire so equipped was the Mark VI, derived directly from the Mark VB as a result of work on pressure cabins at the Royal Aircraft Establishment and Supermarine during 1940-41. At the R.A.E., R7120 was fitted with a Merlin 47 (the high-rated version of the Merlin 45) with a four-blade Rotol airscrew with Jablo blades, and a pressure cabin. The same engine was employed by the 100 Spitfire VI (Type 350) fighters built by Supermarine, the first two of these, AB176 and X4942, serving as prototypes. The production Spitfire VI also had an increase in wing area to improve controllability at high altitudes, the wing being of 'pointed' planform with a span of 40ft 2in. The pressure cabin was contained between the bulkheads fore and aft of the cockpit, and a special non-sliding hood was fitted to simplify the sealing problem. A Marshall blower provided a cabin differential of 2lb/sq.in, reducing apparent altitude from 40,000 feet to 28,000 feet. In other respects, including armament, the Spitfire VI was similar to the Mark VB.[35]

In flight tests, the Spitfire Mk6 attained a top speed of 356mph at 21,800ft. The aircraft achieved a highest altitude of 39,200ft.[36] A total of five RAF squadrons operated Spitfire Mk6s, in the high-altitude interceptor role, from airbases in England from 1942–43.

A developmental Spitfire Mk6 (side view) in January 1942. (US National Archives, College Park, Maryland, Still Pictures Branch)

The developmental Spitfire Mk6 (front view). (US National Archives, College Park, Maryland, Still Pictures Branch)

Production, Flight Testing and Development of the Spitfire Mk7

The Spitfire Mk7 was an advanced version of the Spitfire Mk6, featuring a two-speed Merlin 60 engine. Other design and performance improvements were noted by Green (1965):

> The wing outline remained similar to that of the Spitfire VI, but the ailerons were reduced in span. The chord and area of the rudder were increased and the elevator horn balance was extended. Structural changes were made to the fuselage to take the increased engine loads, and a double-glaze sliding hood was fitted to the cockpit. The retractable tailwheel first developed for the Spitfire III was applied in production for the first time on the Mark VII, and the 'universal' 'C'-type wing was employed. Maximum speed jumped by 44mph to 408mph, and normal loaded weight climbed to 7,875lb.[37]

In 1944, the USAAF obtained Spitfire Mk7 EN474 from the RAF and flight tested it at Wright Field in Dayton, Ohio. In late 1944, NACA Langley obtained the same aircraft for extensive flight research studies. These studies included flying qualities investigations as well as flight experiments aimed at finding solutions to drag problems originating from canvas gun port coverings situated on outer positions on the wings.

Apparently, Mk7 EN474 experienced an accident while at NACA Langley. As stated in an official US Government telegram from Lt J.E. Arnoult, USAAF Materiel Command, Wright Field, Dayton, Ohio, to the commanding general, AAF Technical School, Lowry Field, Colorado, on 15 August 1944:

> AN ACCIDENT TO A SPITFIRE 7 AIRPLANE UNDERGOING TEST BY NACA, LANGLEY FIELD RESULTED IN LOSS OF LANDING GEAR FAIRINGS. REPLACEMENT POSSIBLE FROM SPITFIRE 5 AIRCRAFT. REQUEST INFORMATION AS TO POSSIBILITY OF FURNISHING ONE EACH LEFT AND RIGHT LANDING GEAR FAIRINGS FROM SPITFIRE 5 TO NACA. REPLY BY WIRE TO COMMANDING GENERAL, AAF MATERIEL COMMAND, WRIGHT FIELD, DAYTON, OHIO ATTENTION FOREIGN EQUIPMENT UNIT, TECHNICAL DATA LABORATORY.[38]

A total of 140 Mk7s were produced. Beginning in 1942, Spitfire Mk7s were operational with nine RAF squadrons in England and the Middle East. The Mk7 was unique in that this Spitfire series possessed features that became the norm in later marks. The Spitfire Mk7 EN474 test flown by NACA Langley and Wright Field was restored following the war and is now part of the Smithsonian Institution's vast Second World War aircraft collection on static display at the National Air & Space Museum in Washington DC.

Production, Flight Testing and Development of the Spitfire Mk8

The Spitfire Mk8 was an advanced version of the Spitfire Mk7, but designed for low-altitude use. Three sub-variants were produced, each featuring different engines – the F8 (Merlin 61/63 engine), the HF8 (Merlin 70 engine) and the LF8 (low-altitude Merlin 66 engine). The Mk8 variants were equipped with tropical filters. The F and HF sub-variants featured extended wings, while the LFs used conventional Spitfire wings with huge rudders.

Initial Mk8s became operational in the Middle and Far East. Approximately 1,658 Mk8s were produced.

Flight testing of the Spitfire Mk8 variants showed tremendous gains in speed attained in this version of the Spitfire. In performance trials of a Spitfire F8, JF934 (Merlin 66) conducted at the Royal Australian Air Force Headquarters Directorate of Technical Services, Special Duties and Performance Flight, in January 1944, the aircraft achieved a top speed of 393mph at an altitude of 25,000ft.[39] In additional flight tests, the Spitfire F8 attained its highest speed of 408 mph at 25,000ft. The Spitfire LF8 achieved its highest speed of 404mph at 21,000ft and the Spitfire HF8 attained its highest speed of 416mph at 27,500ft.[40]

Production, Flight Testing and Development of the Spitfire Mk9

By 1942, the German Fw 190As and Bf 109G-6s were showing their dominance over the Spitfire Mk5 variants. Seeking to regain the upper hand, British war planners decided to use a developmental Mk3 Spitfire (N3297) as the prototype of a 'Super Spitfire' design, earmarked to be the most advanced Spitfire designed to date. This 'Super Spitfire' was designated the Mk9 and was outfitted with a Merlin 60 series engine. The aircraft was propelled by a four-bladed Rotol propeller.

The Mk9 was actually produced before (and was slightly slower than) the Mk8. There were three Mk9 variants, designated LF (low-altitude fighter), F (medium-altitude fighter) and HF (high-altitude fighter).

Spitfire Mk7 EN474 in flight over Wright Field on 23 January 1944. (US National Archives, College Park, Maryland, Still Pictures Branch)

Spitfire Mk7 EN474 (side view) on the tarmac at Wright Field on 24 February 1944. (US National Archives, College Park, Maryland, Still Pictures Branch)

Spitfire Mk7 EN474 (front view) at the NACA Langley Memorial Aeronautical Laboratory in late 1944. (NASA Langley Research Center)

Spitfire Mk7 EN474 (front view) on the tarmac at Wright Field on 24 February 1944. (US National Archives, College Park, Maryland, Still Pictures Branch)

Spitfire Mk7 EN474 (rear view) at the NACA Langley Memorial Aeronautical Laboratory in late 1944. (NASA Langley Research Center)

The introduction of the Spitfire Mk9 into combat in July 1942 surprised the Germans. As stated by Green (1965), 'At the usual combat range it was impossible for enemy pilots to distinguish between the Spitfire IX and the inferior Mark V, and this fact gave the British fighter's pilots some tactical advantage at first.'[41]

As the war progressed, the Mk9's armament was enhanced with the incorporation of the 'E' wing in the design in 1944. This enabled a significant jump from the conventional two .303in Browning machine guns to one .5in Browning machine gun positioned in each wing, accompanied by the conventional two 20mm cannon arrangement found in the wings of the later Spitfire Mk5 variants.

Several developmental Spitfire Mk9s participated in important performance and developmental flight tests. Performance trials of a developmental Spitfire F Mk9 (BF274) were conducted at the Aeroplane and Armament Experimental Establishment at Boscombe Down, England on 22 October 1942. The trials were synopsised as follows:

Climb and level speed performance has been measured on Spitfire F. MKIX B.F.274 both with and without a 30 gallon external jettisonable tank fitted. The climb performance at combat rating and position error have also been measured without the tank fitted. The engine was fitted with a 0.477:1 reduction gear and a Rotol R3/4F5/3 metal propeller.

Climb at normal rating:

Maximum rate of climb in M.S. supercharger	3,200ft/min at 13,500ft
Maximum rate of climb in F.S. supercharger	2,540ft/min at 25,900ft
Service ceiling (100ft/min)	42,100ft
Time to 10,000ft	3.1mins
Time to 20,000ft	6.5mins
Time to 30,000ft	10.7mins
Time to 40,000ft	20.2mins

RAF 607 Squadron Spitfire Mk8 being prepped for a mission launched from Mingaladon, Burma, during the Second World War. (Royal Air Force)

The Spitfire Mk8 was the first Spitfire variant to feature a teardrop canopy for enhanced pilot vision. (US National Archives, College Park, Maryland, Still Pictures Branch)

Climb at Combat rating:

Maximum rate of climb in M.S. supercharger	3,860ft/min at 12,600ft
Maximum rate of climb in F.S. supercharger	3,020ft/min at 25,200ft
Service ceiling (100ft/min)	43,400ft
Time to 10,000ft	2.7mins
Time to 20,000ft	5.6mins
Time to 30,000ft	9.2mins
Time to 40,000ft	16.6mins

Level Speeds.

Maximum true air speed in M.S. supercharger	380½mph at 15,400ft	
Maximum true air speed in F.S. supercharger	403mph at 27,400ft	

Without 30 gallon tank [42]

It was also found that the Mk9 could carry bombs and still serve as an effective fighter-bomber. This fact was revealed in flight tests of Spitfire F Mk9 BS428 (Merlin 61) at the Aeroplane and Armament Experimental Establishment at Boscombe Down, England, on 17 March 1943. The flight tests were synopsised as follows:

Level speed measurements have been carried out on this aircraft to assess the effect of fitting a 500lb bomb on an unfaired rack beneath the fuselage. The installation was one designed and fitted by Fighter Command personnel.

Level speed performance was measured between 11,000ft and 21,000ft using all-out level power conditions in M.S. supercharger gear with the radiator flaps closed.

Condition	Max True Airspeed (mph)	Full throttle height (ft)
With one 500lb bomb fitted	363	14,500
With external bomb installations removed	385	14,750

A developmental Spitfire Mk9 (BF273) at Boscombe Down, England, on 27 August 1942. (US National Archives, College Park, Maryland, Still Pictures Branch)

Conclusions

The reduction in maximum true air speed in M.S. supercharger gear due to fitting a 500lb bomb and a bomb rack without fairing is 22mph. [43]

This loss in air speed was considered tolerable and Mk9 performance still adequate to perform ground attack missions successfully. The 500lb bomb was carried beneath the centre fuselage in these trials, and during actual combat missions two 250lb bombs were carried in addition to the centre fuselage-mounted larger bomb, one under each wing.

Recognising the superb air superiority fighter qualities of the Spitfire Mk9, American war planners sought to investigate the aircraft's capability to serve as a long-range escort fighter to accompany Allied heavy bombers deep into the heart of Germany to bomb industrial targets. As a result, two developmental Mk9s were supplied to the USAAF at Wright Field (now Wright-Patterson AFB) in Dayton, Ohio, for special range extension studies in 1944. Highlights and issues encountered during these studies were captured in the following letter, dated 28 July 1944, from USAAC Colonel H.Z. Bogert (acting chief, Engineering Division) to Hap Arnold, commanding general of the USAAF:

Spitfire IX Range Extension Project

1. The modified Spitfire IX airplanes, MK-210 and MK-317, were delivered to Boscombe Down on 11 July 1944. MK-210 departed from Wright Field 4 June 1944 but was delayed in Greenland for approximately thirty days due to damage resulting from engine failure immediately after take-off. MK-317 departed from Wright Field 1 July 1944 and was joined by MK-210 at Greenland for completion of the flight to England. Upon arrival at Boscombe Down both aircraft were delivered to the Commanding Officer of the station.

2. Vicker's [sic] Supermarine has modified a Spitfire IX to increase the combat range by the addition of an aft fuselage tank with 90 gallons capacity and carrying externally a 204 gallon belly tank, the main fuselage tank is standard with the capacity of 104 gallons resulting in an all-up total of 398 gallons. The center of gravity of this airplane with internal fuel only is 11.2 inches aft of the datum line compared with the Wright Field modified Spitfire's center of gravity position of eight inches aft of the datum line in the worst condition. It has been found from operational experience that the maximum external fuel which can be utilised for combat purposes does not exceed 45 percent of the total internal and external fuel supply. Assuming that all of their internal

fuel supply was usable the ratio of 204 gallons carried externally to the all-up total of 398 gallons merely indicates that 50 gallons will be dropped in the belly tank.

3. Flight testing at Boscombe Down of the Vicker's [*sic*] airplane revealed that the ship would not be satisfactory for combat until a minimum of 66 gallons had been burned out of the rear tank leaving an internal fuel supply of 128 gallons. On the other hand, the same Royal Air Force test pilots stated that the airplane modified by Wright Field is satisfactory for combat with the full internal fuel capacity of 196 gallons. The Vicker's [*sic*] airplane is therefore satisfactory with only 128 gallons of fuel. In order to maintain the 45 percent ratio, the maximum fuel that could be carried externally would be 105 gallons resulting in a grand total of 233 gallons. In other words, the British have 'hung on' 398 gallons of fuel out of which only 233 gallons is usable for combat missions. With this amount of fuel the very maximum combat range could not exceed 700 miles as compared with our figure of 1240 miles actually flown.

4. The engineering officials at Boscombe Down were notified on 19 July by the Ministry of Aircraft Production that a decision between the two modifications was to be reached by 24 July. Boscombe Down personnel were in accord with the Project Officer's opinion as stated above. However, it is fairly certain that the official report will favor the Vicker's [*sic*] Supermarine installation.

5. The purpose of this latter is to briefly state facts and figures obtained by the Project Officer in England. A more complete and detailed report will be furnished in the near future.[44]

The controversy surrounding the selection of a long-range extension solution for the Spitfire Mk9 was finally settled when the British Air Ministry later decided to use a mixture of American and British long-range extension methods. This was revealed in the official US War Department letter sent from Colonel J.F. Phillips (chief, Material Division Office, assistant chief of Air Staff, Materiel, Maintenance & Distribution), by command of General Arnold, to General F.O. Carroll (commanding general, Materiel Command, Wright Field, Dayton, Ohio).

Further issues involving these important feasibility flight tests were discussed in another letter, dated 16 August 1944, from USAAC Brigadier General F.O. Carroll (chief, Engineering Division) to Hap Arnold, commanding general of the USAAF:

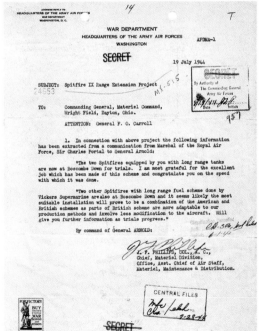

RAF ground crews and a variety of drop tanks, including both drop and slipper tanks, intended for use on Spitfire Mk9s on the 2nd Tactical RAF airfield in England in May 1944. (Royal Air Force)

Official US War Department letter sent from Colonel J.F. Phillips (chief, Material Division Office, asstistant chief of Air Staff, Materiel, Maintenance & Distribution), by command of General Arnold, to General F.O. Carroll (commanding general, Materiel Command, Wright Field, Dayton, Ohio). (US National Archives, College Park, Maryland, Textual Reference Branch)

Spitfire IX Range Extension

1. Enclosed is a copy of a comparative report prepared by Boscombe Down regarding the Spitfire modification. This report is undated and unsigned; however, it was prepared by the Chief Technical Officer, Boscombe Down on 24 July 1944 and was directed to the Ministry of Aircraft Production.

2. The following comments apply to various items contained in the subject report and are submitted in order to clarify a number of questionable points. It is felt that the subject report clearly reflects the official RAF attitude toward the project.

a) In the third paragraph in the introduction a statement is made that it is proposed to fit two additional leading edge tanks similar to those contained in the Spitfire VIII. It is desired to point out that this additional modification would merely serve to make the Vickers airplane somewhat more similar to the Wright Field installation. However, the 85 gallon tank that is installed back of the pilot in the Vickers airplane still is not satisfactory due to the extremely rearward c.g. position. If the Vickers people cut the fuel load that is carried in the rear tank, their installation will then be identical to the Wright Field job.

b) Under paragraph 1, Item 1.2, reference is made to the Wright Field leading edge fuel tank installation. It is stated that 'three adjacent nose ribs have been removed, one of which is of primary structural importance, but there are grave doubts about the strength of the resultant wing structure'. With regards to this statement, Wright Field structures experts are of the opinion that the resultant structure is at least as strong if not more so than a standard Spitfire IX wing. The Project Officer suggested that one of the wings in question should be taken to static test and broken up; however, no action was taken with respect to this suggestion.

   Secondly, it was suggested that it would be entirely possible to utilise production wings from a Spitfire VIII for this modification as they already contain leading edge wing tanks. Approximately 12 gallons of fuel would be sacrificed if this procedure were followed.

c) There are numerous other statements in the Boscombe Down report that are purely of an argumentative nature. A straight-forward comparison of the two airplanes clearly shows the superiority of the Wright Field modification and this superiority has been proved by satisfactory flight test results and satisfactory

A developmental Spitfire Mk9 Mk210 without drop tanks, used in USAAF range extension flight tests at Wright Field on 22 May 1944. (US National Archives, College Park, Maryland, Still Pictures Branch)

Developmental Spitfire Mk9 Mk210 (rear view) with drop tanks, used in USAAF range extension flight tests at Wright Field on 22 May 1944. (US National Archives, College Park, Maryland, Textual Reference Branch)

A view inside the cockpit of the developmental Spitfire Mk9 (Mk210). (US National Archives, College Park, Maryland, Textual Reference Branch)

Spitfire Mk9 Mk210 (side view) with drop tanks. (US National Archives, College Park, Maryland, Textual Reference Branch)

functioning over a long period of time. The Vickers Supermarine Spitfire is still unfinished and remains a very questionable quantity with regard to stability, allowable fuel capacity, and satisfactory operation. The range figures quoted at the last of the subject report are in error. Boscombe Down estimates of the performance of the Vickers Supermarine are compared with actual flight test results on the Wright Field Spitfire, and secondly the Boscombe Down people appear to have confused 'ferry range' with 'combat range'.

3. The purpose of this letter is not solely to criticise the Boscombe Down report; however, it is desired to point out the fact the British have made a hurried attempt to justify their installation to the detriment of the Wright Field installation instead of attempting to pick out the good points of both installations for the purpose of ending up with a satisfactory modification both for production purposes and combat purposes.[45]

As seen in this letter, the USAAF was not pleased with the British apparent disregard for the Wright Field installation, which the Americans found to be more desirable and performance maximising.

A final interesting Mk9 experiment involved the development of a Mk9 floatplane (MJ892) in 1943 by Folland. Like the Mk5b floatplane, the Mk9 floatplane featured an oversized fin to correct instability problems caused by the floats. The Spitfire Mk9 was well-liked by its pilots and along with later Spitfire marks was test flown against a captured Bf 109 G-6. The Mk9 was the most numerously manufactured Spitfire type. Approximately 5,609 Mk9s were produced.

Spitfire Mk11 Development and Usage

The Spitfire Mk11 was specifically developed to test the limits of high-speed and high-altitude flight. The aircraft was intended to be flown at high altitudes and perform high-speed dives to explore the high-speed flight regime approaching the sound barrier as well as the compressibility phenomenon. The Mk11 featured a highly aerodynamic and streamlined nose to perform its important research flights. The airplane made use of a Rotol propeller.

The first research flight was performed by Squadron Leader J.R. Tobin in Spitfire Mk11 EN409 at Farnborough, England, in late 1943. During the flight, Tobin's Mk11 attained a speed of 606mph (Mach 0.891 – the speed of sound is approximately 761mph at sea level) during a dive.

During a later Mk11 test flight on 27 April 1944, Squadron Leader Anthony F. Martindale (RAFVR) experienced a harrowing series of events

Spitfire Mk9 Mk210 (front view) with drop tanks, used in USAAF range extension flight tests at Wright Field on 13 May 1944. (US National Archives, College Park, Maryland, Still Pictures Branch)

An experimental Spitfire Mk9 floatplane performs a water take-off in 1943. (Royal Air Force)

as the Rotol propeller came off in flight. During the dive portion of the research flight, the aircraft attained a speed of Mach 0.92. This was the highest speed achieved by a piston-engined aircraft during the Second World War. The extreme g forces experienced by Martindale caused him to lose consciousness. He later regained his senses with the aircraft at an altitude of 40,000ft. The Rotol propeller popped off during the dive and Martindale proceeded to maintain a glide return to base, arriving with both person and aircraft intact. In recognition of his achievement, Martindale received the Air Force Cross. Thus, the high-flying Spitfire Mk11 gained the notable distinction of having flirted with the sound barrier during the Second World War.

Production, Flight Testing and Development of the Spitfire Mk12

The Supermarine Spitfire Mk12 design combined elements from the Mk5c design and a powerful Griffon 2 engine power plant. The fuselage was reinforced and the wings clipped. In early performance trials, the Mk12 achieved a maximum speed of 393mph. Later flight tests and performance trials of the Mk12 produced even more favourable results.

A listing of the results produced in performance trials of Spitfire F Mk12 DP845 (Griffon 2B) at the Aeroplane and Armament Experimental Establishment at Boscombe Down, England, on 29 November 1942, is as follows:

Spitfire Mk11 EN409. (Royal Air Force)

Summary

Climb Performance

Max rate of climb in M.S. supercharger gear	3,760ft/min at 2,600ft
Max rate of climb in F.S. supercharger gear	2,760ft/min at 15,300ft

Level Speed Performance

In M.S. supercharger gear	372mph at 5,700ft
In F.S. supercharger gear	397mph at 17,800ft[46]

In 1943, the Spitfire Mk12 was fitted with an advanced Griffon 6 engine. Performance trial results from flight tests with this developmental aircraft were as follows:

Summary

Climb Performance

Max rate of climb in M.S. supercharger gear	4,960ft/min at 1,900ft
Max rate of climb in F.S. supercharger gear	4,300ft/min at 10,200ft

Level Speed Performance

In M.S. supercharger gear	375mph at 4,600ft
In F.S. supercharger gear	389mph at 12,800ft[47]

Mk12s became operational with RAF 41 and 91 Squadrons and served in the interceptor role protecting the British Isles. When German V-1 'Doodlebug' flying bombs were first launched by Germany in 1944 against British civilian targets, it was the Mk12s that rose to the defence of England to eliminate the new threat that was striking fear in the minds of the British populace. A total of 100 Spitfire Mk12s were produced.

A Spitfire Mk12 in flight. (United States Air Force)

RAF 41 Squadron Spitfire F Mk12s in flight. (Royal Air Force)

Production, Flight Testing and Development of the Spitfire Mk14

In 1943, Supermarine sought to incorporate the powerful Griffon 65 engine in a yet more advanced Spitfire design. Their solution was to use a Mk8 base design and reinforce it structurally to accommodate the hulking engine power plant. The new design was designated the Spitfire Mk14 and featured a new five-blade Rotol propeller. An oversized vertical tail was added to the design along with a 'C' wing weaponry arrangement.

Some later Mk14 variants utilised the 'E' wing and a teardrop canopy for enhanced piloting vision. A photo-reconnaissance variant of the Mk14, designated the FR14E, was also produced.

Performance trials of the Mk14 (Spitfire Mk8 Conversion JF319 – Mk14 prototype) proved to be encouraging, particularly in the significant increase in speed, as reflected in flight tests at the Vickers-Armstrong Ltd Supermarine Works conducted on 10 September 1943. The results were summarised as follows:

Summary of Results

At the all up weight for the Spitfire XIV i.e. 8400lb and at 18lb/sq.in and 2,750rpm, the results are:

Maximum level speed in F.S. gear, 447mph at 25,600ft

Maximum level speed in M.S. gear, 389mph at 6,000ft[48]

Similar results were recorded in flight tests of the same test aircraft (equipped with a Griffon RG5SM engine) at the Aeroplane and Armament Experimental Establishment at Boscombe Down on 27 October 1943:

(i) On the climb at combat rating:

Max rate of climb in MS supercharger gear   5,040ft/min at 2,100ft

Max rate of climb in FS supercharger gear   3,550ft/min at 22,100ft

(ii) In all-out level flight:

Max true air speed in MS supercharger gear   391mph at 5,500ft

Max true air speed in FS supercharger gear   446mph at 25,900ft[49]

A British test pilot boards the first Spitfire Mk14e (RB140) prior to taking off on a flight test at the de Havilland factory, Hatfield, Hertfordshire, England, in March 1944. (US National Archives, College Park, Maryland, Still Pictures Branch)

The first Mk14s became operational with RAF 610 Squadron on 1 January 1944. The Mk14 carved its place in history by becoming the first Allied aircraft to shoot down a German Me 262 jet fighter. This feat was accomplished by an RAF 401 Squadron Spitfire Mk14 over north-western Europe on 5 October 1944. The Mk14 was also highly effective in disposing of V-1 flying bombs. Numerous Mk14s became operational with RAF units in the Pacific theatre toward the end of the Second World War.

Approximately 1,055 Mk14s were produced.

Production and Development of the Spitfire Mk16

In 1944, the British Air Ministry and war planners sought an advanced version of the Spitfire to serve in a ground-attack capacity. The solution was found in the form of the Spitfire Mk16, derived from the Mk9 and featuring a Packard Merlin 266 engine power plant as a replacement for the Mk9's Merlin 61 engine.

Initial Mk16s also featured 'C' wing weaponry and most Mk16s had clipped wings. Later Mk16s featured 'E' wings and had a teardrop canopy for enhanced piloting vision.

Spitfire Mk14e RB140 during flight trials in March 1944. (US National Archives, College Park, Maryland, Still Pictures Branch)

A developmental/test teardrop canopy-equipped Spitfire Mk14 (rear top view) in flight in December 1944. (US National Archives, College Park, Maryland, Still Pictures Branch)

Spitfire Mk14e RB140 flashes its underside during flight trials in March 1944. (US National Archives, College Park, Maryland, Still Pictures Branch)

A developmental/test teardrop canopy-equipped Spitfire Mk14 (rear side view) in flight in December 1944. (US National Archives, College Park, Maryland, Still Pictures Branch)

A German Messerschmitt Me 262 jet fighter being examined by service members of the 5th Armoured Division (US Ninth Army) in an abandoned Luftwaffe hangar at an airfield close to Stendal, Germany, on 5 April 1945. (US National Archives, College Park, Maryland, Still Pictures Branch)

A captured German Messerschmitt Me 262 jet fighter at Wright Field in September 1945. (United States Air Force)

Mk16s became operational with the RAF 2nd Tactical Air Force in 1944. Also in 1944, a developmental/test Spitfire Mk16 participated in tests of a new air-to-ground rocket projectile installation system, known as the Mk8 Type 3 RP Installation Air-to-Ground Weapons System.

Approximately 1,054 Spitfire Mk16s were produced.

Production and Development of the Spitfire Mk18

Following the development of the Spitfire Mk14, Supermarine sought to build on the successful Mk14 design and structurally reinforced it. In addition, fuel tanks were added in both the wings and back portion of the fuselage. The new aircraft became known as the Spitfire Mk18 and some variants (the FR and F18) were equipped with cameras mounted in the fuselage for photo-reconnaissance duty.

Just 300 Mk18s were manufactured, and the majority of these were slated for duty in the Far East. However, none of these aircraft ever saw action during the war.

A captured German Messerschmitt Me 262 jet fighter on a test/evaluation flight above Wright Field in September 1945. (United States Air Force)

A developmental/test Spitfire Mk16 in flight. (US National Archives, College Park, Maryland, Still Pictures Branch)

A developmental/test Spitfire Mk16 equipped with Mk8 Type 3 air-to-ground rockets. (United States Air Force)

Production, Flight Testing and Development of the Spitfire Mk21

Toward the end of the Second World War, the British Air Ministry was seeking a replacement for the highly successful Spitfire Mk14. This replacement became known as the Spitfire Mk21, and by May 1945 the Air Ministry put in a request for 3,000 of these aircraft. Early flight tests of Mk21s produced promising results. The results of performance tests of the prototype Spitfire F Mk21 DP851 (Griffon 61 engine) conducted at the Vickers–Armstrong Ltd Supermarine Works on 27 May 1943 were as follows:

Summary of Results

At an all-up weight of 9,000lb and with combat rating of 2,750rpm and 18lb boost:

a) Maximum level speed   455mph at 25,600ft
b) Maximum rate of climb   4800ft/min at 7,700ft
c) Time to 30,000ft   7.85mins
d) Service ceiling   42,800ft
e) Coolant and oil suitabilities: Full tropical under combat climb conditions.[50]

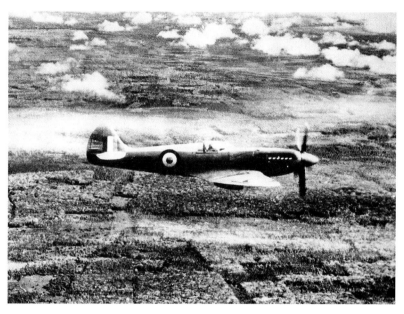

A developmental/test Spitfire Mk18 in flight. (US National Archives, College Park, Maryland, Still Pictures Branch)

In addition, performance tests of the second prototype Spitfire F Mk21 PP139, on 10 September 1943, indicated an increase in speed of 5mph compared to earlier tests. The results of these tests, also conducted at Vickers–Armstrong Ltd Supermarine Works in England, were as follows:

A developmental Spitfire Mk21 (rear top view) in flight in November 1944. (US National Archives, College Park, Maryland, Still Pictures Branch)

Summary of Results

At an all up weight of 9,070lb and under engine conditions of 18lb/sq.in and 2,750rpm, the results are:

(a) Maximum level speed in F.S. gear, 460mph at 25,600ft

(b) Maximum level speed in M.S. gear, 432mph at 12,200ft[51]

However, as pointed out by Ivan Rendall in *Spitfire: Icon of a Nation* (2008), the Mk21 suffered from several operational problems that hindered its immediate mass production and deployment to frontline RAF squadrons:

When it had been tested by pilots of the Air Fighting Development Unit in December 1944, there were signs that the great Spitfire tradition might be drawing to an end. It was difficult to fly: take-off required full port rudder trim to counter-act the starboard yaw induced by the power of the engine; once airborne, the pilot had to adjust the rudder trim rapidly while also coping with a highly sensitive elevator control and establish a steady climb while adjusting trim and gathering speed from below 180mph, at low level, which took very high levels of concentration. Even at 25,000 feet it was an uncomfortable aircraft to fly: rudder movements created instability in the horizontal plane which, if unchecked, developed into a corkscrewing motion, making formation flying and accurate gunnery difficult. The RAF test pilots gave their view that technically there was little to choose between the Mk.21 and the Mk.XIV it was intended to replace, and that in combat, the Mk.XIV was the better all-round fighter.[52]

Nevertheless, these operational issues were overcome with modifications to the aircraft's tail and rudder, specifically making them oversized. As a result, Mk21s became operational with RAF 91 Squadron in April 1945, disposing of mobile V-2 rocket launching units in northern Holland before the end of the war in Europe. The V-2 rocket was the world's first ballistic missile used by Hitler and the Nazis to destroy British and Allied populace centres throughout Europe during the latter years of the Second World War. Spitfire Mk21s were used much like American USAF F-15E Strike Eagles were used to take out mobile SCUD missile launchers during Operation Desert Storm in 1991.

Only 120 Spitfire Mk21s were produced.

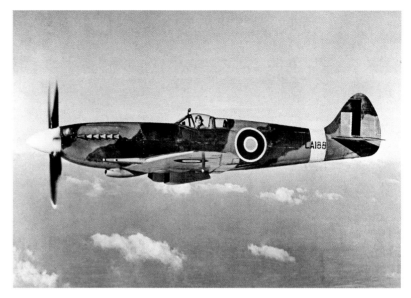

Developmental Spitfire Mk21 LA188 (side view) in flight in November 1944. (US National Archives, College Park, Maryland, Still Pictures Branch)

Developmental Spitfire Mk21 LA188 (front view) in flight in November 1944. (US National Archives, College Park, Maryland, Still Pictures Branch)

Developmental Spitfire Mk21 LA188 (three-quarters front view) in flight in November 1944. (US National Archives, College Park, Maryland, Still Pictures Branch)

A Spitfire Mk21 takes off from a British airfield in 1945. (US National Archives, College Park, Maryland, Still Pictures Branch)

A Spitfire Mk22 in flight. (US National Archives, College Park, Maryland, Still Pictures Branch)

Developmental Spitfire Mk21 LA188 flashes its underside in flight in November 1944. (US National Archives, College Park, Maryland, Still Pictures Branch)

Development and Operational Use of the Spitfire Mk22

The Supermarine Spitfire Mk22 was developed immediately following the Second World War and was essentially a further advancement of the Mk21 design. Mk22s served with only one RAF squadron. They were eventually relegated to Auxiliary Air Force service.

Production and Development of the Spitfire Mk24

The Supermarine Spitfire Mk24 was the final Spitfire variant produced. Only eighty were manufactured. These became operational with RAF 80 Squadron in Germany, serving until July 1949. RAF 80 Squadron later transferred to Hong Kong, flying its Mk24s through January 1952. Thus ended the legendary Spitfire's reign in the skies.

PHOTO-RECONNAISSANCE SPITFIRE VARIANTS

Production, Development and Operational Use of the Spitfire PR Mk1a

During the initial years of the Second World War, the British Air Ministry and war planners requested that Supermarine convert some of its Spitfire Mk1s into photo-reconnaissance variants to keep tabs on the progress of the German military in the build-up to and during the Blitzkrieg. The result was the Spitfire Photo Reconnaissance (PR) Mk1a. This aircraft was outfitted with a special camera to perform its important mission. Mk1as became operational with the RAF Special Survey Flight unit in France in November 1939. Later Spitfire Mk1 photo-reconnaissance versions included the PR Mk1b, PR Mk1c, PR Mk1d, PR Mk1e, PR Mk1f, and PR Mk1g.

Each sequential progression of the PR Mk1 variant featured an improvement in operational range, made possible by the addition of fuel tanks and advances in fuel storage through aircraft structural modifications, as well as more advanced cameras and camera types.

Two hundred and twenty-nine PR Mk1ds were manufactured. These were developed into PR Mk4s.

A developmental Spitfire Mk24 PK713 (front view) at Boscombe Down, England, in January 1947. (US National Archives, College Park, Maryland, Still Pictures Branch)

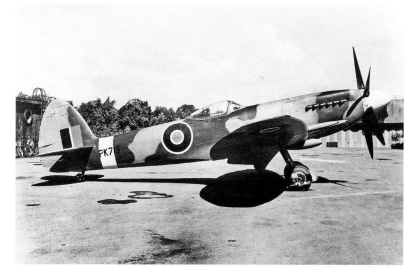

A developmental Spitfire Mk24 PK713 (side view) at Boscombe Down, England, in January 1947. (US National Archives, College Park, Maryland, Still Pictures Branch)

Development and Use of the Spitfire PR Mk4

The Supermarine Spitfire PR Mk4 was developed from the Spitfire PR Mk1d in 1941. The PR Mk4 made use of the Merlin 45 engine and featured fuel tanks in the wings and a heated cockpit for long-range, high-altitude missions. PR Mk4s served with the RAF Photo Reconnaissance Unit (PRU). One of their primary missions with the PRU was to conduct surveillance flights over ports in France and Norway in an attempt to track the locations and activities of the German warships in the Atlantic that posed a grave threat to Allied merchant fleets.

Development and Use of the Spitfire PR Mk11

In November 1942, an advanced Spitfire PR version was produced. This version became known as the PR Mk11 and was evolved from the Spitfire Mk9. The aircraft was outfitted with a Merlin 61 engine that boosted its high-altitude capability. However, PR Mk11 pilots suffered from the lack of a pressurised cockpit in the design. Spitfire PR Mk11s performed important damage survey missions following Operation Chastise, the famous Avro Lancaster Dam Buster missions, devised and orchestrated by Guy Gibson and RAF Bomber Command, carried out against large dams in Germany in May 1943.

Development and Use of the Spitfire PR Mk13

In 1943, a more advanced version of the PR Mk11, the PR Mk13, was produced. The PR Mk13 was designed for low-altitude missions, but was equipped with oblique cameras. PR Mk13s performed numerous survey flights, scoping out desirable D-Day landing sites in France for Allied forces.

Development and Use of the Spitfire PR Mk19

In 1945, Supermarine produced a Spitfire PR version, designated the PR Mk19, outfitted with the powerful Griffon engine. The PR Mk19 was truly a specimen of aerodynamic excellence. Sleek PR Mk19s performed numerous important tactical photo-reconnaissance missions toward the end of the Second World War, as Allied forces advanced through the German countryside.

A developmental Spitfire PR Mk11 (EN654) in flight, with test pilot Jeffrey Quill at the controls. (Imperial War Museum, E (MOS) 1325)

NAVALISED SPITFIRE VARIANTS: THE SEAFIRES

Production, Flight Testing and Development of the Seafire Mk1b

In 1941, Britain's Fleet Air Arm (the Royal Navy) sought a navalised version of the Spitfire for fighter operations aboard aircraft carriers. The navalised version of the Spitfire, dubbed the 'Seafire', was evolved from a Spitfire Mk5b. The Mk5b was modified by adding an A-frame arresting hook.

Carrier suitability trials were conducted aboard HMS *Illustrious*. These trials were so successful that forty-eight Seafires were requested by the Royal Navy. These converted Spitfire Mk5bs were designated Seafire Mk1bs and were modified by Air Service Training at Hamble. The Seafire Mk1b also had a structurally reinforced fuselage.

Soon, the Royal Navy's Seafire Mk1b fleet grew, exceeding 100 in quantity. Seafire Mk1bs became operational with Royal Navy 807 Squadron aboard HMS *Furious*, and played a crucial role in helping Britain and its allies maintain air superiority over the strategic Mediterranean island of Malta.

Interestingly, the first aerial victory scored by a Seafire was a Vichy French Dewoitine D520 downed over the beach during the Allied invasion of North Africa in November 1942.[53]

Production, Flight Testing and Development of the Seafire Mk2c

In 1943, the Supermarine Seafire Mk2c rolled off the assembly line. This Seafire variant was essentially a modified Spitfire Mk5c. A total of 262 Seafire Mk2cs were produced.

Seafire Mk2cs featured various Merlin engines ranging from the 45 to the 56. A few Seafire Mk2cs, designated Seafire L Mk2cs, employed Merlin 32 engines complete with Rotol four-blade propellers. Early flight tests of a developmental Seafire Mk2c (MA970, Merlin 46 engine) conducted at the Aeroplane and Armament Experimental Establishment at Boscombe Down in October 1942 proved to be promising:

Summary

Performance on the climb and in level flight has been measured on this aeroplane with and without a 30 gallon under-fuselage fuel tank of the type that can be dropped when empty. A 4-blade Rotol propeller was fitted.

A summary of the results obtained follows:-

	Without 30 gal tank	With 30 gal tank
Take-off weight (lb)	7,145	7,425
Max rate of climb (ft/min)	2,380 at 16,000ft	2,200 at 16,000ft
Time to reach 10,000ft	4.25mins	4.6mins
Time to reach 20,000ft	8.55mins	9.35mins
Time to reach 30,000ft	15.65mins	17.5mins
Service ceiling at 3,000 rpm	37,500ft	36,300ft
Estimated absolute ceiling at 3,000 rpm	38,400ft	37,200ft
Max true airspeed in mph	342 at 20,700ft	332 at 20,700ft

Partial climb tests gave a best climbing speed of 150mph to 16,000ft reducing 2mph per 1,000ft thereafter.

Engine rpm was changed on the climb from 2,850 to 3,000 at 25,000ft.

1. Introduction

Performance on climb and in level flight were required on this aeroplane both with and without a 30 gallon fuel tank fitted beneath the fuselage. These tests were made with a temperate air intake and it was intended to make comparative trials with a tropical intake fitted; however, due to the aeroplane being required elsewhere urgently, the latter tests could not be made.

5. Discussion of results.

It will be seen from the results that the effect of fitting the 30 gallon fuel tank lowers the maximum rate of climb by 180ft/min, the service ceiling by 1,200ft, and the maximum true air speed by 10mph.

The 24th Part of Report No. A.&A.E.E./692i dealt with similar tests of effect on performance of fitting a 90 gallon external tank to a Spitfire Vb. The changes in performance obtained now and on these previous tests are approximately in the expected proportion.

It is estimated from recent tests on a Spitfire Vc aeroplane, (results of which are about to be issued) that the fitting to a universal wing of 2 x 20mm Hispano guns and 4 x .303 machine guns instead of the 4 x 20mm Hispano guns as fitted in this case, would give an increase in speed of approximately 3mph true air speed.

There is not sufficient evidence available to enable the reduction in performance due to fitting a tropical air intake with air cleaners to be estimated accurately.

The increase in performance obtainable by using combat rating (+16lb/sq.in boost; 3000rpm) on a Spitfire Vc is given in the 38th Part of Report No. A.&A.E.E./692i, and this increase will approximately apply equally to the Seafire.[54]

Early flight tests of a developmental Seafire L Mk2c (MB138, Merlin 32 engine) conducted at the Aeroplane and Armament Experimental Establishment at Boscombe Down in late February 1943 were also encouraging:

1. Introduction.

The climb and speed performance has been measured on Seafire L Mk.IIC MB138, fitted with a Merlin 32 engine. The climb performance was measured using normal and combat power ratings.

2. Condition of aircraft relevant to tests.

2.1 General. The principal features of the aircraft are given below:-

A Merlin 32 engine
A 4-blade propeller, type V.P RF/4F5/4
Triple ejector exhaust stubs with fishtails and heater stubs.
The heater tubes were not connected at the rear of the exhausts.
Ice guard over air intake which was of the temperate type.
Universal wings as on Spitfire VC.
Armament:- 2 x 20mm guns, 4 x 0.303" machine guns; relevant ejection chutes open; 20mm gun muzzles and 0.303" gun ports sealed. Hemispherical blanks over remaining 20mm gun stubs.
Catapult spools beneath and on the sides of the fuselage.
Rear view mirror above the windscreen.
Internal bullet proof windscreen.
Wireless mast behind cockpit.
W/T aerial.
No I.F.F. aerials
A 30 gallon auxiliary drop tank was not fitted during these tests.

3. Scope of tests.
The following tests were made:-

i) Partial climbs at heights of 5,000ft and 29,500ft at combat rating and at 6,000ft at normal rating to determine the best climbing speed.
ii) One climb at combat rating using the best climbing speed from test (i) with the radiator exit duct flap fully open.
iii) One climb at normal rating using the best climbing speed from test (i) with the radiator exit duct flap fully open.

It was found necessary to increase the climbing speeds in order to obtain satisfactory cooling results at normal rating, and the climbs were therefore repeated using the speeds as follows:-

iv) Two climbs at combat rating at increased climbing speed with the radiator fully open.
v) Two climbs at normal rating at increased climbing speed with the radiator fully open.
(Combat rating is normally permitted for periods of 5 minutes only, but for test purposes full climbs were allowed at this rating).
vi) Level speeds at heights between ground level and 27,000ft with the radiator exit duct flap in the minimum drag position.

4. Results of tests.
The results have been corrected to standard atmospheric conditions by the methods given in Report No. A& A.E.E./Res/170. The level speeds have been corrected to 95% of the take-off weight, i.e. 6,645lb by the method given in the same Report.

The position error used was that given in the 38th Report No.A& A.E.E./692,i. for a Spitfire V. A.A.878, which had the same type of wing, armament and pressure head installation as this aircraft.

In correcting the speed measurements a 'strut correction' has been applied in addition to the usual position error and compressibility corrections, the source of this correction being the A.R.C. Report 6420.

i) The best climbing speed found from the partial climbs was 160mph A.S.I. up to 6,000ft (approximately full throttle height at normal rating) decreasing by 1½mph per 1,000ft thereafter, for both normal and combat rating.

In view of the adverse cooling results obtained at this climbing speed, the climbing speed was increased to 180mph A.S.I. up to 6,000ft, decreasing by 2mph per 1,000ft thereafter.

The decrease in rate of climb obtained by increasing climbing speed was small and within the experimental scatter observed for the rate of climb curves given in this Report.[55]

After performing carrier suitability trials, it was found that the Seafire L Mk2c possessed underwhelming carrier take-off capability. To boost this capability, the Royal Navy decided to equip all Seafires with Rocket Assisted Take-Off Gear (RATOG). Seafire 2s were used by the Royal Navy in support of the Allied campaign for Sicily.

Production, Flight Testing and Development of the Seafire Mk3

In the next version of the Seafire, the Mk3, the wings folded for ease of stowage aboard aircraft carriers as well as the ability to accommodate and operate more aircraft from the ships. The Spitfire Mk5c was used as a base design for the Seafire Mk3.

Initial performance trials of the first production Seafire Mk3 (LR765, Merlin 50 engine) conducted at the Aeroplane and Armament Experimental Establishment at Boscombe Down in August 1943 proved to produce adequate results for Royal Navy officials:

Introduction.

Seafire III LR.765 was the first production Mk.III, made by Messrs Westland Aircraft Ltd, and was sent to this Establishment for brief check handling and performance trials. This part of the Report deals with the climb and level speed performance.

Results of similar tests made on Seafire II Mk.970 have been reported in the 2nd Part of Report No. A.&A.E.E./785,a.

★ ★ ★

3. Scope of tests.

Climbs were made at normal rating to 34,000ft with the radiator exit duct in the fully open position, using a climbing speed of 150mph ASI up to 16,000ft, and decreasing by 2mph per 1,000ft thereafter. These climbing speeds were those determined for Seafire II MA.970, reported on in the 2nd Part of Report No. A.&A.E.E./785,a.

Maximum level speeds were measured at heights up to 26,000ft with the radiator exit duct flap in the minimum drag position.

4. Results of tests.

The results of the climb and level speed performance tests have been corrected to standard atmospheric conditions by the methods given in Report No. A.&A.E.E./Res/170, and the results of the level speeds have been corrected to 95% of the take-off weight, viz. 6,750lb by the method given in the same Report. A 'strut correction' based on ARC.6420 has also been applied and the compressibility correction has been calculated by the methods given in the Addendum to Report No. AAEE/Res/147. The position error has been taken from the 38th Part of Report No. A.&A.E.E./692,i. on Spitfire VC AA.878, which had similar pressure head installation.

An operational Royal Navy Seafire Mk2c makes an arrested landing aboard a British carrier on 1 March 1944. (US National Archives, College Park, Maryland, Still Pictures Branch)

A developmental/test Seafire Mk2c performs a RATO from a simulated British carrier deck on 11 July 1944. (The New York Times/Redux, US National Archives, College Park, Maryland, Still Pictures Branch)

Rocket Assisted Take-Off (RATO) apparatus on a developmental/test Seafire Mk2c on 11 July 1944. (US National Archives, College Park, Maryland, Still Pictures Branch)

The results of the climb performance tests are given in Table I and Fig.1, and those of the level speed performance tests in Table II and Fig.2. A brief summary of the results is given below:

Climb Performance

Max rate of climb at sea level	2,500ft/min
Max rate of climb at 14,200ft (FTH)	2,600ft/min
Max rate of climb at 20,000ft	1920 ft/min
Max rate of climb at 30,000ft	745ft/min
Service Ceiling	35,600ft
Estimated absolute ceiling	36,200ft

Level Speed Performance

Maximum true airspeed at 4,000ft	321mph
Maximum true airspeed at 10,500ft (FTH)	351mph
Maximum true airspeed at 24,000ft	328mph

Conclusions

Tests similar to these were made previously on Seafire II MA.970 and reported in the 2nd Part of Report No. AAEE/785,a. Brief tests subsequently made on the same aircraft after it had been converted to a Mk.III by fitting folding wings showed the speed performance to be unchanged. No strict comparison between the results of these tests and those obtained on MA.970 is, however, possible, as MA.970 was fitted with a Merlin 46 engine. The two engines are, however, similar in power out-put under comparable conditions, and the performance of LR.765, the aircraft now tested, is slightly better than that of MA.970. It is therefore concluded that the performance of this first production aircraft is satisfactory.[56]

Approximately 350 Seafire Mk3s were produced by Cunliffe-Owen Aircraft. An additional 948 Seafire Mk3s were manufactured by Westland Aircraft. Two Seafire Mk3 variants were produced – the FR3 and the LF3. The FR3 was used primarily for photo-reconnaissance missions and was accordingly equipped with a vertical camera and an oblique camera located in the fuselage. Some LF3s were outfitted with Merlin 45 engines, while others were outfitted with Merlin 32 engines.

Carrier suitability trials to determine whether Seafire Mk3s could be operated from US aircraft carriers were conducted at the Naval Air Station Patuxent River, Maryland, in late 1943 and early 1944 using a large simulated aircraft-carrier deck turntable (see p. 59), equipped with carrier-arresting wires.

A British Royal Navy developmental/test Seafire Mk3 at NAS Patuxent River, Maryland, prior to carrier suitability trials on 9 December 1943. (US National Archives, College Park, Maryland, Still Pictures Branch)

The developmental/test Seafire Mk3 (front view) prior to carrier suitability trials on 13 December 1944. (US National Archives, College Park, Maryland, Still Pictures Branch)

The Seafire Mk3 (rear view) prior to carrier suitability trials on 13 December 1944. (US National Archives, College Park, Maryland, Still Pictures Branch)

A British Royal Navy Seafire Mk3 in flight in September 1944. (US National Archives, College Park, Maryland, Still Pictures Branch)

British Royal Navy Mk3 Seafires perform practice strafing attacks on USS Catoctin *(AGC 5), and in the process provide simulated target practice for shipboard anti-aircraft gunners during amphibious exercises conducted in the waters near Arzew, Algeria, on 11 June 1944. (US National Archives, College Park, Maryland, Still Pictures Branch)*

A British Royal Navy Firefly, Seafire Mk3 and Avenger aboard a British escort carrier serving as part of the British Pacific Fleet deployed in the waters near Sakishima Gunto in April 1945. (US National Archives, College Park, Maryland, Still Pictures Branch)

Production, Flight Testing and Development of the Seafire Mk15

In 1944, the new advanced and powerful Griffon 6 engine was incorporated in the latest Seafire design. This marriage of technology resulted in the superb Seafire Mk15. Seafire Mk15 development mirrored Spitfire Mk12 development. A notable distinction between the Seafire Mk15 and earlier Seafires was the addition of a 'sting hook' to replace the obsolescent arresting gear found on earlier versions of the Seafire. Handling trials of the prototype Seafire Mk15 (NS487) conducted at the Aeroplane and Armament Experimental Establishment at Boscombe Down in March 1944 produced glowing results. They were as follows:

1. Introduction.

The Seafire F.Mk.XV is a naval development of the Spitfire F.Mk.XII and is fitted with a Griffon VI engine, folding wings, and deck landing equipment. Apart from an enlarged rudder balance tab and an additional radiator beneath the port wing there is very little aerodynamic difference between the two

types of aircraft, though it is understood that later aircraft will have a curved windscreen and 'tear drop' sliding hood. NS.487, the first prototype Seafire F.Mk.XV was sent to this Establishment for handling trials which included the determination of the aftmost acceptable centre of gravity position. The results of these tests are dealt with in this Part of the Report.

2. Condition of aircraft relevant to tests.

2.1   General. The principal features of the aircraft were:-

A Griffon VI engine.
A 4-blade Rotol hydraulic propeller type R13/1P5/6.
Individual ejector exhaust stubs.
No ice-guard over air intake, which incorporated an alternative intake with an air cleaner.
Radiator under starboard wing, and radiator and oil cooler under port wing.
2 x 20mm guns and 4 x 0.303" guns fitted, muzzles and leading edge ports sealed and ejection chutes open.
Folding wings with bulge over 20mm mechanism, and folding tips.
Deck-landing arrestor hook beneath fuselage.
Retractable tail-wheel and link-type undercarriage.
Whip aerial above fuselage with aerial wire to fin.
Type 91 aerial below starboard wing.
Balloon hood.
Circular rear view mirror with fairing above windscreen.

The finish of the aircraft was very good. The skin was flush-rivetted throughout, all joints were filled with compound, and the whole aircraft was polished to give a smooth surface.

The aircraft was fitted with the latest type of elevator having increased horn balances (11 balance). The rudder had a combined balance and trimmer tab, this tab being larger than that fitted on earlier marks of Seafire and Spitfire; details are given in Fig.2.

3. Scope of tests.

General handling tests were carried out at each of the loadings of para. 2.2 to assess the flying qualities of the aircraft; an assessment of the cockpit layout and view for deck landing has also been made.

Brief routine tests were carried out at loadings (2) and (3) along the lines given in AP.970, Chap. 903 to determine the aftmost acceptable centre of gravity position, the aircraft being fitted with a stick force indicator and a visual accelerometer. With the aircraft trimmed into dives the stick forces and accelerations during recovery were noted at speeds up to 450mph ASI; and with the aircraft trimmed for high speed level flight (engine conditions 2600rpm +9lb/sq.in boost), the push force required to hold the aircraft in dives up to 450mph ASI and normal acceleration following release of the control column were noted.

With the aircraft trimmed for level flight at approximately twice stalling speed the pull forces required for 4g turns in either direction were noted, and the pull forces were also noted in turns at from 1 to 5g in increments of 1g with the aircraft trimmed for high-speed level flight.

4. Results of tests.

4.1   Cockpit layout. The layout of the cockpit was substantially the same as that in the Spitfire XII and only the following points required comment:-

Constant reading petrol gauges were fitted in place of the usual push-button type. The gauges were easy to read and appeared to be reasonably accurate, though no precise checks were carried out.

An emergency method of flap operation was not provided, though it was understood that this was to be incorporated in all Seafire aircraft. The provision of such a system is most desirable.

It was not possible to dim the lights indicating the position of the tail wheel and arrestor hook, and it is felt that some dimming would be desirable for night operation.

The addition of a small lever to the throttle friction lock knob was an improvement.

Handling characteristics at loading (1).

4.21 Take-off. The taxiing qualities of the aircraft were normal and the view on the ground was not appreciably altered by the larger nose as compared with earlier Seafire marks.

Using +9lb/sq.in boost and full left rudder trim take-off was straightforward, and the tendency of the aircraft to swing to the right when the throttle was opened could be easily held by a moderate foot load on the rudder bar. When using the normal +15lb/sq.in boost the tendency to swing was greater but the aircraft could be held straight without undue difficulty, the foot load required being heavy but not excessive. There was a marked drop of the right wing due to torque reaction, but though this was slightly uncomfortable it was not serious.

The tail rose easily and the aircraft left the ground after a short run, followed by a good initial climb away.

4.22 Controls.

Elevator. The elevator displayed the normal characteristics of the type. It was slightly heavy throughout the speed range with engine on, this being particularly noticeable at low airspeeds with high powers. The elevator hunted slightly at low speeds in rough air conditions. These minor defects are typical of the elevator with enlarged horn balance and have been commented on in several other reports.
   When gliding with flaps and undercarriage down the elevator was very light over the mid-part of its range, but become considerably heavier when large control movements were made.

Rudder. The fitting of the increased area balance tab has affected a considerable improvement in rudder control when compared with the Spitfire F Mk.XII. The rudder was effective throughout the speed range and was very light at low speeds. The control became heavier as speed increased, but remained reasonably light for the small movements normally used at high speeds.

The changes of directional trim with speed and power could be easily held on the rudder bar without retrimming.

Ailerons. The ailerons displayed the normal characteristics for an aircraft of the Spitfire type, though the set fitted to NS487 were rather heavy. The weight of the control increased considerably with speed, and above 400mph ASI the ailerons were excessively heavy.

4.23 Stability.
Longitudinal. An assessment of the longitudinal stability characteristics from the general handling tests made was that this feature was satisfactory under

all conditions of flight, though the aircraft was noticeably less stable under climbing or gliding (flaps and undercarriage up) conditions than at higher speeds. The stick free stability appeared large by comparison with the stick fixed stability, since, following a disturbance in 'hands off' flight the restoring motion appeared to come from the action of the elevators.

The phugoid characteristics were briefly:-

On the climb – one or two oscillations followed by speed decreasing to the stall.

Level flight at slow cruising speeds and faster – a return to trimmed condition through damped oscillation.
Glide flaps and undercarriage up – oscillation increasing in amplitude.
Glide flaps and undercarriage down – undamped oscillation.

None of the phugoids were violent in character.

4.24 Stalling characteristics. With flaps and undercarriage up the aircraft stalled at 80mph ASI, showing the usual Spitfire characteristics.

With flaps and undercarriage down the stalling speed was 68mph ASI, the stall being normal except for a slight twitching of the ailerons just before the stall occurred.

4.25 Dives. Trimmed for all-out level flight the aircraft was dived to 450mph ASI. The aircraft was steady in the dives and the push force required to hold the aircraft in the dive increased with speed, becoming heavy at the maximum speed attained. When the control column was released the aircraft recovered quickly without showing any tendency to tighten up automatically or produce excessive normal accelerations during recovery.

Recovery from a trimmed dive was quick and the pull force required was moderate, the aircraft showing no tendency to tighten up automatically during recovery.

It was noticed that the wing-folding doors lifted slightly during the dives.

Further remarks on the dive characteristics are given in para. 4.4.

4.26 Aerobatics. All normal fighter aerobatics were carried out and the behaviour of the aircraft was found to be satisfactory.

4.27 Approach and landing. Simulated deck landings were carried out on both a runway and a grass airfield without the assistance of a batsman.

The view forwards for landing is considered to be somewhat better than that on other marks of Seafire aircraft, the improvement being due to the fitting of the single ejector exhausts in place of the broad triple ejectors employed on earlier Seafire aircraft.

Approaches were made at 75mph ASI, but at 80mph ASI the aircraft was more comfortable to fly, and the pilot had more control over the attitude and rate of descent. Compared with earlier marks of Seafire it was more difficult to control the approach speed and the lack of drag was more noticeable. The difficulty of speed control was probably due to the fact that only small throttle movements were required for considerable increases in power, and hence it was rather difficult to check the sink without either increasing the approach speed or causing a nose-up change of attitude.

On this particular aircraft the harmony of the controls was poor at low speeds; the ailerons being rather heavy and the elevator and rudder very light.

This type of aircraft seems suitable for operation from aircraft carriers and deck landing should present no more difficulty than on Seafire aircraft at present in service.

4.3   Handling characteristics at loadings (2) and (3). The flying characteristics at these loadings were generally similar to those at loading (1), but the following points were noted:-

4.31 Take-off. The take-off was normal, but 1–1½ divisions more nose down elevator trim than at loading (1) was required. The tail rose quickly, very little force being required on the control column. The tendency to swing was very little different from that previously experienced. On the initial climb the aircraft felt slightly less stable than previously and the elevator tended to hunt somewhat more at low speeds.

★ ★ ★

The prototype Seafire Mk15 (front view) at the Aeroplane and Armament Experimental Establishment at Boscombe Down in March 1944. (US National Archives, College Park, Maryland, Textual Reference Branch)

The prototype Seafire Mk15 (rear view). (US National Archives, College Park, Maryland, Textual Reference Branch)

The prototype Seafire Mk15 (side view). (US National Archives, College Park, Maryland, Textual Reference Branch)

An operational British Royal Navy Seafire Mk15 in flight in December 1944. (US National Archives, College Park, Maryland, Still Pictures Branch)

British Royal Navy Seafire Mk15 in flight (front view) in December 1944. (US National Archives, College Park, Maryland, Still Pictures Branch)

British Royal Navy Seafire Mk15 in flight (rear view) in December 1944. (US National Archives, College Park, Maryland, Still Pictures Branch)

British Royal Navy Seafire Mk15 in flight (rear side view) in December 1944. (US National Archives, College Park, Maryland, Still Pictures Branch)

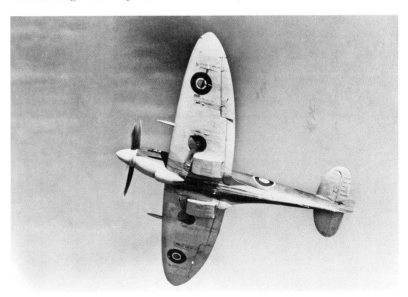

British Royal Navy Seafire Mk15 in flight (underside view) in December 1944. (US National Archives, College Park, Maryland, Still Pictures Branch)

Conclusions.

The aircraft is considered to be suitable for carrier operation and no undue difficulty should be experienced. The swing to the right at take-off can be easily held on the rudder, and normal deck-landing technique can be used, though this is slightly more difficult than on previous Seafire aircraft.[57]

Approximately 134 Seafire Mk15s were produced by Cunliffe-Owen. An additional 256 Seafire Mk15s were manufactured by Westland.

Production and Development of the Seafire Mk17

The Seafire Mk17 was developed in late 1944 and was essentially similar to the Seafire Mk15, but the conventional bubble type canopy was replaced with the more pilot friendly teardrop canopy. Approximately twenty Seafire Mk17s were produced by Cunliffe-Owen with an additional 169 Seafire Mk17s being manufactured by Westland.

Production, Flight Testing and Development of the Seafire Mk47

The final version of the Seafire produced, the Mk47, rolled off the assembly line following the Second World War and was essentially a navalised version of the Spitfire Mk22, but featuring a contra-rotating pair of three-blade propellers. Flight trials of a developmental Seafire Mk47 (PS957) detached to the Naval Air Fighting Development Unit at the Central Fighter Establishment at RAF West Raynham, England, in May 1949 proved that the aircraft was of sound aerodynamic design and well-suited for combat operations. The results of these flight trials were as follows:

I. INTRODUCTION

1(3) The Seafire 47 is a single seat low wing monoplane fighter and fighter bomber. It is powered with a Rolls Royce Griffon 87 or 88 engine driving a Rotol 6 blade, constant speed, contra propeller. The aircraft carries 152 gallons of internal fuel in 7 tanks, all of which are self-sealing with the exception of the upper fuselage tank. In addition, the aircraft can carry a 22½ gallon combat tank under each wing and a 50 gallon drop tank under the fuselage, giving a total fuel capacity of 247 gallons.

II. GENERAL AND FLIGHT CHARACTERISTICS.

II(1) Engine Starting. The starting technique as laid down in Pilots' Notes has been found satisfactory. It is stressed, however, that the engine may be easily over primed. On full stroke of the priming pump is all that is required for a 'cold' start except in extremely cold weather. The engine takes 1½–2 minutes to reach its minimum take-off temperature on an average winter's day in this country.

II(2) Handling on the Ground. The aircraft is easy to taxi; little recourse to the brakes is necessary, except when manoeuvring in confined spaces; forward view is however, very poor and constant weaving is necessary in order to see ahead.

II(3) Handling in the Air. At low speeds, in the 'clean condition' the controls are very sensitive in the pitching plane. In particular, in the climb, when the emptying of the rear fuselage tank and the opening of the radiator flaps induce changes of longitudinal trim, the pilot's attention is constantly required

An operational British Royal Navy Seafire Mk17 in flight. (US National Archives, College Park, Maryland, Still Pictures Branch)

in keeping the aircraft in an accurate climbing attitude. In general flight at medium altitudes and for aerobatics, the Seafire 47 handles in much the same way as previous marks of Seafire, with the exception, in the case of the 47, that due to the contra-prop there is very little alteration of rudder trim with changes of power and speed.

The handling qualities of the aircraft at high altitudes are reasonably good, but above 32,000' it is difficult to maintain a really effective climbing attitude. Trouble has also been experienced at high altitudes with the stiffening of the controls, particularly the ailerons. Violent lateral movement of the control column from the controls quickly; but they begin to stiffen up again almost immediately afterwards.

When flying with the rear fuselage tank full, the aircraft shows a marked tendency to tighten up in turns; and at high altitudes, with or without the rear tank full this 'tightening up' tendency is noticeable.

There is considerably more vibration in the 47 than that encountered on earlier marks of Seafire; it occurs at nearly all engine powers but is particularly noticeable at low RPM and high boost conditions.

The cockpit of the Seafire 47 is small, and a large pilot is forced to sit in a hunched attitude, which although ideal for combat, becomes uncomfortable on long sorties. The positioning of several of the controls, in particular the fuel cocks and Grid ring of the compass is such that they cannot be reached without loosening the safety harness. The safety harness release is awkwardly positioned, being situated too high and too far aft in the cockpit to be accessible. Considerable physical effort is required to reach this control.

The instructions laid down in Pilots' Notes for the management of the fuel system are satisfactory, but nevertheless complicated; and very considerable thought is required by the pilot on this point, particularly when wing combat and drop tanks are fitted. On low flying sorties it is vital that the pilot should keep a very close watch on his fuel state. Should the pilot be flying on the rear fuselage or drop tank and either tank inadvertently run dry; the time required to release the harness, lower the seat and reselect the awkwardly attached fuel cocks may cause him to lose flying speed before the engine picks up again.

There is no cockpit heating either thru that indirectly derived from the engine and on prolonged sorties at high altitude the cockpit becomes uncomfortably cold.

11(4) Take-off and Landing. Take-off in the 47 is easier than in previous marks of Seafire, since there is no tendency to swing. The landing presents no new problem except for the very marked drop of the nose if power is taken off quickly.

11(5) Instrument and bad weather flying. The Seafire 47 is uncomfortable to fly in 'bumpy' conditions; in particular the rudder is very sensitive and it is very easy to over-correct. In addition, the forward view is very poor, particularly in low visibility when it is necessary to make continuous 'S' turns in order to see ahead.

Instrument flying is quite satisfactory and all the instruments, with the exception of the engine speed indicator are visible with the seat fully lowered and up to the half raised position; with the seat any higher the top half of the instrument panel is obscured.

The de-icer is satisfactory and will clear moderate ice formation from the front panel of the windscreen.

11(6) Night flying. The aircraft has not been flown under completely dark conditions, but several flights at dark showed that exhaust glare would make night flying difficult; since even at dark the exhausts present a blinding glare to the pilot. The red cockpit lighting at present fitted is satisfactory, but U.V. lighting would be desirable if the aircraft were to be used regularly at night.

11(7) Low flying. The aircraft is very manoeuvrable, but the very poor forward view makes low flying and pin-pointing difficult, in all but the fairest weather.

11(8) Pilot navigation. The cramped conditions in the cockpit make the operation of a plotting board uncomfortable and difficult. Maps have to be carried in the leg pocket of the pilot's flying suit since no stowage is provided in the aircraft.

When flying at low airspeeds, via flying for range, the increased angle of attack further restricts the already poor forward view and limits pin-pointing to objects fine on the how or on the quarter.

11(9) Misting. The de-mister is only partially effective; although it will keep the inside of the front windscreen clear, it has no effect on the side panels which mist up completely when descending rapidly from altitude. Rubbing the panels with the glove clears them temporarily but the mist soon reforms; flying around at low altitude for 5–10 minutes is usually necessary to clear them satisfactorily.

A layer of ice may also form on the inside of the panels and this can take anything up to 10 minutes to clear. Opening the canopy at low altitudes will assist in dispersing either mist or ice. It is recommended that the hot air de-mister be made to operate on all windscreen panels and not the front one only. The canopy does not appear to be susceptible to misting.

II(10) <u>Conclusions</u>.

i)   The Seafire 47 handles much the same as previous marks of Seafire; the cockpit is however more cramped and pilot fatigue is considerable on long sorties.

ii) The aircraft has a good high altitude performance, but the cockpit heating is inadequate for prolonged flights at high altitude.

iii) Exhaust glare makes the aircraft unsuitable for night operations.

iv) Misting of the windscreens is a serious handicap if a rapid descent is made from high altitude, which could be remedied by the provision of heating on the side panels.

v)   The engine speed indicator is difficult to read in its present position.

★ ★ ★

III. TACTICAL CHARACTERISTICS.

III(1) N.A.C. Form 101 for this trial does not call for a complete report on this aircraft in all its roles; but a brief summary of the main characteristics is made below.

III(2) <u>Combat flying</u>. In common with previous marks of Seafire the 47 is a good combat aircraft and is very manoeuvrable. Its chief advantage over earlier marks is due to the contra rotating propellers which almost entirely eliminate the need for changes of rudder trim with speed. This considerably reduces the chances of skid whilst in the curve of pursuit or dive and should make it a more accurate gun platform.

Its chief disadvantage is in its poor forward view, for whilst having a slightly greater angular view over the nose than some earlier marks, the double sandwich bullet proof glass and curved Perspex windscreens reduce forward visibility and make flying in all but the fairest weather unpleasant and also considerably reduces the search view.

III(3) <u>Formation flying</u>. The 47 is pleasant to fly in formation, the response to throttle movements being very positive if the RPM are kept around 2400.

III(4) <u>Harmonisation</u>. The 50 yard alignment diagram for the Seafire 47 was issued in this Unit's report 154/NAMU/192 of 18th February, 1949. The R/P sight settings which were the subject of a separate trial will now be included in the Final Report.

III(5) <u>Re-arming</u>. The re-arming drill for this aircraft is given in Appendix H of this report.

III(6) <u>Conclusions</u>. The Seafire 47 is suitable for use in most fighter and fighter bomber roles, but not as a night fighter. Its high altitude performance and manoeuvrability make it the best high altitude fighter of all the piston engine aircraft now in service.[58]

A total of ninety Seafire F Mk47s and Seafire FR Mk47s were produced by Supermarine. Seafire Mk47s were used primarily in the fleet defence and ground-attack roles during the Korean War, serving with 800 Squadron aboard HMS *Triumph* in 1950. The Seafire was officially retired from active duty in 1951 and the great Supermarine Spitfire/Seafire lineage faded into history.

A developmental Seafire Mk46, the Mk47 predecessor variant, flashes its underside in flight in 1950. (US National Archives, College Park, Maryland, Still Pictures Branch)

The prototype Seafire Mk47 (side view) at the Aeroplane and Armament Experimental Establishment at Boscombe Down in January 1947. (US National Archives, College Park, Maryland, Still Pictures Branch)

The prototype Seafire Mk47 (front view). (US National Archives, College Park, Maryland, Still Pictures Branch)

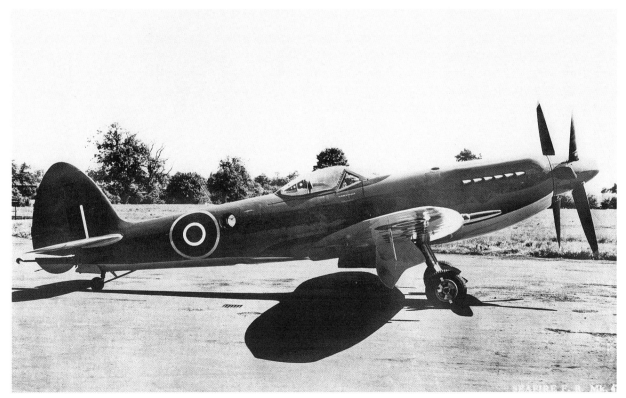

A developmental British Royal Navy Seafire Mk47 (side view) at the Aeroplane and Armament Experimental Establishment at Boscombe Down during the late 1940s. (US National Archives, College Park, Maryland, Still Pictures Branch)

TRAINER SPITFIRE VARIANT

Production, Development and Use of the Spitfire TR9

Following the Second World War, Supermarine pursued the development of Spitfire trainers to help better train RAF and foreign pilots on learning the basics of Spitfire and Seafire operations. The first post-Second World War attempt at designing a Spitfire/Seafire trainer involved the use by Vickers of a Spitfire Mk8 (MT818) as a base design, which was built up into a trainer. The Spitfire Mk9 was later used as the basis for a Spitfire/Seafire trainer and designated Spitfire TR9.

Ten TR9s were delivered to India to be used by its air force in 1948. Six TR9s were also used by the Irish Air Corps (IAC) in 1951 to train their prospective Seafire aircrews. The TR9s flown by the IAC possessed two .303 Browning machine guns.

DEVELOPMENTAL FLIGHT TESTING AFFECTING ALL SPITFIRE MARKS

Flight Testing Designed to Resolve the Great Debate – To Fly with 'Clipped' or Conventional Wingtips?

In 1942, a unique series of flight tests were conducted, using various marks of Spitfire and Seafire, at the Aeroplane and Armament Experimental Establishment at Boscombe Down to determine which was better to fly with – 'clipped' or conventional wingtips. The scope and results of these tests were as follows:

1. Introduction.

Each of the following aircraft have been flown at this Establishment with and without wing tips:-

Spitfire Vs	A.A.937 and A.B.186
Spitfire IX	B.S.139
Spitfire XIIs	E.N.221 and E.N.222

RAF Spitfire TR9 (front view) in May 1947. (US National Archives, College Park, Maryland, Still Pictures Branch)

RAF Spitfire TR9 (rear view) in May 1947. (US National Archives, College Park, Maryland, Still Pictures Branch)

In addition a Seafire III has been flown with and without wing tips.

This report sums up the principal features of the two conditions, and includes remarks on both handling and performance. Some performance results have already been issued (see 44th part of Report No. A.&A.E.E./692,i.) but are reiterated again to complete the comparison.

2. Condition of aircraft relevant to tests.

2.1   General. The main features of the aircraft tested are given in the following table:

Mark	Vb	Vb	IX	XII	XII
Number	A.A.937	A.B.186	B.S.139	E.N.221	E.N.222
Engine	Merlin 46	Merlin 46	Merlin 61	Griffon II	Griffon II
Propeller	D.H.45/4	Rotol RX5/10	Rotol R3/4P5/3	Rotol R13/4P5/6	Rotol R13/4P5/6
Wings	Normal Vb	Normal Vb	Universal	Universal	Universal
Armament	2x20mm guns	2x20mm guns	2x20mm guns	2x20mm guns	2x20mm guns
	4x 0.303" guns	4x 0.303" guns	4x 0.303" guns	4x 0.303" guns	4x 0.303" guns
Unusual features	–	Modified horn balanced elevator	–	–	–

Each of these aircraft were flown with normal and clipped wings. When clipped, the wing span was reduced from 37ft to 32ft 6in, and the wing area from 242sq.ft to 231sq.ft. A plan form and photographs of the clipped wings were given in the 45th part of Report No. A.&A.E.E./692,i.

2.2   Loadings. The aircraft were flown at the following loadings:-

Aircraft	Mk No.	Weight (lb)	Dist. of C.G. aft of Datum point (ins)
A.A.937	Vb	6,540	8.2
A.B.186	Vb	6,535	8.2
B.S.139	IX	7,445	4.4
E.N.221	XII	7,400	5.7
E.N.222	XII	7,335	5.4

2.3   Aileron rigging. The aileron droop was measured on Mk.Vb A.A.937 on arrival, when it was found to be zero. This was then adjusted to give the correct droop of ⅜in droop.

3. Description of tests.

The first Spitfire aircraft with clipped wings to be tested by this Establishment was A.A.937, a Mk.Vb. This aircraft carried out comparative performance and handling tests with normal and clipped wings. The aileron control on this aircraft was above the average in that it was light and effective at high speed. Accordingly, further comparative handling tests were made on Spitfire IX B.S.139 which was known to have rather poor aileron control in that it was heavy and sluggish. At the same time arrangements were made to send A.A.937 to the R.A.E. for stiffness tests of the aileron circuit, to ensure that it was not abnormal.

At this time a proposal that all Mk.XIIs should be fitted with clipped wings was under discussion, and to obtain data on this point, and also to obtain further general information on handling qualities, two Spitfire XII aircraft, E.N.221 and E.N.222, were flown by a number of pilots both with and without wing tips. A few attempts to measure times to bank were made on these aircraft.

The handling tests included not only a qualitative measurement of the rate of roll, but also observations of the characteristics in dives, medium and tight turns, at the stall, during aerobatics and at take-off and landing.

In order to check the effect on the indicated airspeeds on a given aircraft due to changes in position error when the wings were clipped, a further aircraft,

A.B.186 (Mk.Vb) was fitted with a special A.S.I. system, the pitot-static head being fitted on the front of one of the 20mm gun barrels. Readings of this A.S.I. together with the normal A.S.I. were taken over a range of speeds, stalling speeds being noted in particular.

In addition to these tests, take-off tests with normal and clipped wings have been made on the Vb A.B.186, and also on a Seafire aircraft on which 18° of flap were available for take-off.

The tests were made between November, 1942 and February, 1943.

4. Results of tests.

4.1   Handling. Initially handling tests were made on A.A.937, special attention being paid to rolling characteristics. It was found that there was little appreciable difference between the rolling characteristics of this aircraft with tips on and off. The aileron control on this aircraft was, however, above the average for the type, although subsequent stiffness tests at the R.A.E. showed the aileron circuit to be normal. It was thought that any difference in rolling qualities might be more obvious on an aircraft with poor ailerons and hence tests were made on the Mk.IX B.S.139. Here again, however, little appreciable difference could be discerned between the qualities with tips on and off.

More thorough tests were subsequently made on the two Mk.XII aircraft. An attempt was made to obtain some quantitative indication of the rolling qualities by measuring the time to roll from 30° of bank on one side to 30° of bank on the other side, the pilot applying as much aileron as he could as quickly as possible.

The results are plotted in Fig.1, and they indicate that on E.N.221, which had poor ailerons, there was quite an appreciable decrease in the time to bank when the tips were removed. On E.N.222 the ailerons were better than those of E.N.221 with normal or clipped wings, and in this case there was no appreciable difference in the qualities. The pilot's impressions were that the weight of the controls was not changed when the tips were removed, but a given control movement was slightly more effective.

In general manoeuvres, the normal wings were very much superior. With clipped wings the aircraft could not turn as fast or as tight, and in mock combat was easily out-turned by the aircraft with normal wings. The stalling speed in turns was considerably higher with the clipped wings and this aircraft also tended to become unsteady at a higher speed above its stall.

4.2   Stalling speeds. The following stalling speeds were observed:-

Aircraft	All-up weight	Wings	Stalling speeds – mph ASI	
			Flaps & u/c up	Flaps & u/c down
Mk.V. A.B.186	6,535lb	Normal	72	62
		Clipped	80	66
Mk.XII. E.N.221	7,400lb	Normal	75	Not obtained
		Clipped	93	72
Mk.XII. E.N.222	7,335lb	Normal	76	63
		Clipped	90	74

The Mk.V A.B.186, and one of the Mk.XII aircraft were dived to 450mph A.S.I. when fitted with clipped wings. The aircraft remained steady in the dive, and no signs of buffeting developed.

As already explained some tests were made with a special additional A.S.I. system fitted to A.B.186, the position error of which would be unaffected by the change in tip shape. These tests indicated that the difference between the equivalent air speeds with and without wing tips would be about 2mph less than the difference between the normal A.S.I. readings.

It will be seen that removing the wing tips produced a much larger change in stalling speed on the Mk.XII than on the Mk.V. We can offer no satisfactory explanation of this discrepancy, but merely record the results obtained. The only feature which appreciably differed were the additional stubs and bulges for the 20 mm. guns on the Mk.XII wings, and the difference in design and direction of rotation of the propeller.

It is pointed out that the change in stalling speed that might be expected due to the reduction in wing area is only about 2mph.

The stalling characteristics with and without wing tips were very similar in each case.

4.3   Take-offs and landings. The take-off and landing characteristics were unaffected by removing the wing tips. No change in the length of the runs was apparent to the pilots, but there was a noticeable change in A.S.I. at take-off (see table below) which may be a position error affect aggravated by the proximity of the ground. Analysis of the films taken during measured take-offs show only a small change in true air speed.

The results of measured take-offs corrected to zero wind and standard atmospheric conditions are summarised below:-

	Spitfire V A.B.186		Seafire III A.M.970	
	Normal	Clipped	Normal	Clipped
Flaps	Nil	Nil	18°	18°
Take-off run – yards	262	270	229	252
Distance to 50ft screen – yards	–	–	500	530
A.S.I. at take-off – mph	–	–	70	75
True air speed at take-off – mph	89	89	88	89

The above Seafire III results were given in the 2nd part of Report No. A.&A.E.E./785,b.

4.4   Performance. The performance results obtained on A.A.937 are summarised in the following table. The results were given fully in the 46th part of Report No. A.&A.E.E./692,i.

	Normal wings	Clipped wings
Maximum rate of climb (at 15,200ft)	2,840ft/min	2,670ft/min
Time to 10,000ft	3.7mins	3.9mins
Time to 20,000ft	7.4mins	7.9mins
Time to 30,000ft	13.6mins	15mins
Service ceiling	38,000ft	36,200ft
Maximum speed at 17,000ft	342mph	343mph
Maximum speed at 19,800ft (F/T height)	353mph	353mph
Maximum speed at 25,000ft	346mph	342mph

5. Conclusions.

From the foregoing paragraphs the advantages and disadvantages of removing the wing tips appear to be:-

Advantages.

i)   A small increase in the rate of roll of aircraft with originally poor ailerons, but little effect on aircraft with good ailerons.

ii)   A slight increase in speed at heights below about 20,000ft

This captured Bf 109G-6 Gustav in British markings, shown at the Eighth Air Force Station 167 in England on 25 April 1944, was flown against numerous Allied aircraft, including late war Spitfires, in mock aerial combat. (US National Archives, College Park, Maryland, Still Pictures Branch)

Disadvantages.

i)   An inability to turn as fast or tight as an aircraft with normal wings due to an increased stalling speed in the turn, thereby detracting considerably from the fighting efficiency of the aircraft.

ii)   A small increase in take-off run (only serious on ship-borne aircraft).

iii)   A loss in maximum rate of climb at any height of 160–200ft/min.

iv)   A lowering of the service ceiling by 1,800ft.

v)   A decrease in speed above 20,000ft.

In view of these facts, and in particular of disadvantage (i), it is recommended that the wing tips are not removed from Spitfire aircraft.[59]

Fly-offs between Late War Spitfires and a Captured German Bf 109G-6 Gustav

In April 1944, a captured German Bf 109G-6 Gustav was test flown against several late war Spitfires at the 8th Air Force Station 167, England. This USAAF station was the home of the 381st Bomb Group. The fly-offs between the captured Gustav and the late war Spitfires showed that the British aircraft severely outmatched and outperformed their German foe in simulated combat.

5

SPITFIRE EFFECTIVENESS IN COMBAT

The Supermarine Spitfire was a highly versatile fighter, capable of performing a variety of missions. The Spitfire served as a highly effective bomber buster, ground attack fighter-bomber, aerial photo reconnaissance platform, night interceptor, and fighter escort for Allied heavy bombers, in addition to excelling in the aerial dogfighting arena. The Spitfire quickly became a maker of aces during the Second World War, while earning the respect of the enemy.

COMBAT EFFECTIVENESS OF THE SPITFIRE AS AN AIR SUPERIORITY FIGHTER

The excellent air superiority fighter characteristics of the Spitfire were demonstrated on countless occasions during the Battle of Britain and its prelude. On many of these occasions, RAF Spitfire MkI pilots used the overwhelming performance superiority of their Spitfires over German aircraft, both fighters and bombers, to down numerous enemy aircraft and squelch the impending threat of Operation Sea Lion. One such account, in the skies over Dunkirk, was described by RAF Spitfire MkI Pilot Officer John Freeborn of Flight A, 74 Squadron, on 24 May 1940:

I was flying as No.2 Red Section 'A' Flight No. 74 Squadron. Whilst on Patrol A.A. fire was noticed and we saw a formation of 9 HE.111s flying West at 12,000 feet followed by another formation of approximately 12 to 15 HE.111s and DO.17s. We were flying at 500 feet when A.A. fire was first noticed and we climbed to 12,000 in line astern. As we came into range of the second wave, Red Leader ordered 'Echelon Port'. I then attacked a HE.111 and got a two seconds burst in, starting at, and finishing at 100 yards. Due to a large overtaking speed I had to break away. As I broke away, two ME.109s got onto my tail and I dived steeply with the two enemy aircraft following me, one was on my tail and the other on my port quarter. As I dived to ground level I throttled back

Above: Evidence of the excellent dogfighting characteristics of the Spitfire – this severely damaged Me 109E-3, downed by a Spitfire Mk1, was publicly displayed in the main square in Bolton, Lancashire, during the Battle of Britain. (US National Archives, College Park, Maryland, Still Pictures Branch)

Opposite: In this gun-camera still, a German Heinkel He 111 medium bomber sustains machine gunfire damage in its port engine from an RAF Spitfire Mk1 during the Battle of Britain. (Imperial War Museum, CH 1830)

RAF Spitfire Mk1 undergoes rearming and servicing by ground crews at an RAF airfield in England during the height of the Battle of Britain in September 1940. (Royal Air Force)

A Spitfire Mk1 pilot rotation during the Battle of Britain at Colerne, Wiltshire. For the majority of the Battle of Britain, the situation for the RAF was perilous and the threat of German invasion, in the form of Operation Sea Lion, was imminent. The RAF was being destroyed on the ground via intense aerial bombing of airfields and industrial targets by the Luftwaffe, as well as experiencing a loss and shortage of experienced fighter pilots. This situation changed, however, when Adolf Hitler decided that the Luftwaffe should target British population centres instead. This shift in strategy enabled the RAF to rearm and recover, and establish air superiority over the British Isles denying Germany this advantage so essential to mounting a successful invasion. (Imperial War Museum, CH 2821)

slightly and the enemy aircraft on my tail over shot me and I was able to get a three seconds burst at a range of about 50 to 100 yards. He seemed to break away slowly to the right as though he was badly hit and I think he crashed. The second ME.109 then got onto my tail but I got away from it by using the boost cut out.[60]

The Spitfire's superiority over the Me 109 and obsolescent Junkers Ju 87 dive-bomber was displayed when Flight Lieutenant John Webster of RAF 41 Squadron, flying a Spitfire Mk1, encountered large formations of these aircraft over England on 29 July 1940. Webster described the action in his official combat report as follows:

I was leading Green Section No. 41 Squadron to engage enemy fighters over Dover. I was acting as look-out section when I saw several ME-109s approaching. I warned Mitor Leader and attacked a 109, opening at 200 yards and closing to 50 yards. I saw the aircraft catch fire and spin down. I then looked around for further aircraft attacking the squadron. I saw the ME-109 spin down very flat, on fire, amid ships, and hit the sea near the South Goodwin Lightship.

I then saw a squadron of JU-87s dive bombing. I joined on the end of the line diving on Dover and I attacked the end aircraft giving a five second burst from 250 yards to 50 yards. The aircraft was hit and smoke started to emerge, but, during this attack I was engaged by three or four further 109s. I turned to attack these but on getting into a position for a full deflection shot I pressed the 'tit' and nothing happened. (No more Ammo.) I continued to make attacks at the 109s, whilst losing height to sea level.

On reaching sea level I used twelve boost and made for the coast. Seeing that my aircraft was damaged I brought it back to Hornchurch.

Aircraft crashed on landing.[61]

The Spitfire's bomber-busting capability was once again displayed two days following the commencement of the Battle of Britain on 15 August 1940, when Flight Lieutenant George Gribble (Blue Leader) of RAF 54 Squadron met up with a large formation of Ju 87s. As he stated in his combat report:

The Squadron was ordered to engage enemy aircraft in the Dover area. I sighted a large number of Ju 87s in line astern (7000 feet) dive bombing between Hawkinge and Dover.

I dived to the attack, using 12 boost, and fired a long burst at one from astern. It seemed to 'shudder' in mid-air and then dived away steeply with black smoke coming from it. I saw my ammunition entering the machine. By this time I had

RAF Spitfire Mk5c performing a take-off aboard USS Wasp *en route to providing air superiority support over Malta in May 1942. (United States Navy)*

An RAF 132 Squadron Spitfire Mk5b, piloted by Sqn Ldr J.A.F. MacLachlan, blasts a German Ju 88 medium bomber out of the sky near Paris, France. (Imperial War Museum, C 3805)

lost my section and climbed up inland through 5/10 cloud, but did not see any further enemy aircraft and so returned home.[62]

In March 1942, a small force of Spitfires and Seafires, comprised of Spitfire Mk5bs and Mk5cs, and Seafire Mk3s, was delivered to the British island fortress of Malta in the Mediterranean, to defend the island from relentless Luftwaffe and Regia Aeronautica (Italian air force) attacks. This small fleet of Spitfires and Seafires and their pilots heroically helped to maintain British possession of this strategically important island as well as helping to preserve possession of the important island of Gibraltar. Had the Axis nations gained control of these islands they could have mounted air raids on important Allied military bases and forces in North Africa, the Middle East and the Mediterranean. In addition, the Axis nations would have been able to launch extensive aerial resupply missions to aid General Erwin Rommel and the Africa Corps in North Africa and German/Italian forces in the Middle East and Mediterranean.

So confident in the capabilities of the Spitfire was the USAAF leadership that they assumed command of all three Eagle Squadrons, all of which were equipped with Spitfire Mk5bs operating from airbases in England, on 29 September 1942. The Eagle Squadrons were absorbed by the US Army Eighth Air Force and became known as the 4th Fighter Group. Before receiving this honour, however, they gained distinction and praise serving the RAF.

The Eagle Squadrons' best performance was recorded during the Dieppe Raid, in which they showed up in force, in 1942. During intense fighter sweeps over the Dieppe area, Eagle Squadron 71 Spitfire Mk.Vbs destroyed a Junkers Ju-88, while an Eagle Squadron 121 Spitfire shot down a Focke Wulf Fw-190. Eagle Squadron 133 Spitfires destroyed another four Fw-190s, along with a Ju-88 and Dornier Do 217. At the time the Eagle Squadrons were absorbed into the USAAF, they had recorded the destruction of 73½ German aircraft. These figures are a testament to the tremendous capability of the Spitfire as an air superiority fighter.

When the Spitfire Mk9 was introduced into combat in 1942, it had a profound effect on the morale of its pilots as well as in combat on the enemy. This was revealed in the first combat action recorded by RAF 64 Squadron, operating from RAF Hornchurch, from 28–30 July 1942. As stated in the report:

28/7 After a noisy night when 70 Huns raided Birmingham and we got ten destroyed, three probables and ten damaged it turned out a lovely day and a Rodeo was put on at 1210 hours. All four Squadrons [64, 122, 81, and 154] took part. Rendezvous was made at Pevensey Bay and then to St Valery where we

Transfer of Command ceremony of the American Eagle Squadron from the RAF to the USAAF on 29 September 1942. Brigadier General F.O.D. Hunter, Commanding General Fighter Command American Forces, presents Eagle Squadron pilots with US Wings badges in commemoration of the unit command transfer. Major G.A. (Gus) Daymond (second from left) served as commander of an Eagle Squadron and participated in fighter sweeps over the Dieppe area. Major C.W. McColpin (far right), a resident of Buffalo, New York, served as commander of another Eagle Squadron, and became a famous Eagle Squadron Ace, responsible for the destruction of nine German aircraft. (The New York Times/Redux, US National Archives, College Park, Maryland, Still Pictures Branch)

American Eagle 2 Squadron Spitfire Mk5bs head out in formation on a fighter sweep over German-occupied France. (AP Images)

jettisoned our tanks at 20000 feet and then climbed to 31500 feet by the time we got to Le Havre. Nothing was seen save four 190s going back into France at 11000 feet when we were coming out at Fecamps and we were too high to do anything about it. One of 81 Squadron [Sgt Moston] had to make a belly landing near Hawkinge through lack of petrol. So ends our first operation with Spitfire IX's.

29/7 Very dull cloudy weather till it cleared at 1600 hours. The other three Squadrons [340, 81, 122] sent two pairs each on Rhubarb operations from which two aircraft of 81 Squadron did not return. The four new Sergeants were put through their paces in the afternoon and after about six landings in a Spit V Sgt Brooker flew a Spit IX and put up a very good show by landing in good order when his tire burst on his third take-off.

30/7 Lovely fine day after a very noisy night with Hun bombers dropping bombs at Barnet. A Circus on Abbeville was put on at 1140 hours and we were top Squadron, at 25000 feet in a Diversionary Wing to St Omer. Nothing was seen till after we had left France at Le Touquet when we had a perfect jump on nine FW 190s. Unfortunately, just as we were about to attack, Controller warned us a Typhoon had just been shot down and would we make quite certain they were 190s – this just put everyone off their stride and F/L Kingaby was the only one to get a Destroyed which crashed on the outskirts of Boulogne. On his return 'Kingo' [F/L. Kingaby] was greeted with the news that he was posted within 24 hours to the Middle East but this was cancelled in the evening.

At 1820 a Ramrod came on to Dunkirk with us top squadron as usual to the wing of four squadrons. Halfway between the French Coast and St Omer when we were at 15000 feet [3,000ft a minute in Spitfire MK9s is some climb!] we saw about 15 FW 190s below and 'Smithy' [Sqn Ldr Smith] led the squadron down to attack. As a result of the superior performance of the Spit IX [and pilots!] the Hun was properly bounced again and S/L. [Sqn Ldr] Smith, Stewart and Michael Donnet got one destroyed apiece, W/C [Wing Commander] Finlay who was flying with us got a damaged, and Stromme and Ullestad had two squirts which, if substantiated by cameras with which we are not yet fitted, might easily have led to a claim. On the way back 'Smithy' and Austeen saw a Spit having a dogfight with a 190 4000 feet below so they just joined in the fun and games and shot it down in flames about 8 miles off Calais. Five destroyed in one day is not bad. The rest of the wing lost eight including S/L. Leon Prevot from 122 Squadron which is hard luck – Prevot is the third C.O. [commanding officer] 122 has lost in three months.[63]

The exemplary combat effectiveness of the Spitfire as an air superiority fighter was once again demonstrated during the Spitfire Mk12's first foray in combat in 1943. As described by Mike Williams and Neil Stirling on their excellent internet website spitfireperformance.com, 'Spitfire Mk XII Performance – Brief Operational History':

The first operational sorties with the Spitfire XIIs occurred on 3 April, Form 541 noting, 'Scramble base at Valley to 27,000ft. Nothing to report'. Intensive operations, however, began after the squadron moved to Hawkinge on 13 April. 41 Squadron took over the duties of 91 Squadron, which went off operations and moved to Honiley to also re-equip with Spitfire XIIs. F/O [flying officer] R.H.W. Hogarth drew first blood, shooting a Ju-88 down into the sea 2 miles North of Ostend on 17 April. On 27 April Blue Section engaged 4 FW 190s while carrying out a recco to Calais-Somme. F/O C.R. Birbeck downed one of the FW 190s, thus marking the Spitfire XII's first confirmed victory against a German fighter. Operational duties for April

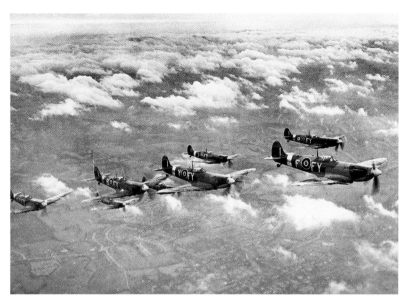

RAF 611 Squadron Spitfire Mk9s form up on their way to escort USAAF B-17 heavy bombers in August 1942. (United States Air Force)

RAF Polish Squadron early Spitfire Mk9 in November 1942. (Royal Air Force)

Two RAF 241 Squadron Spitfire Mk9s return to base after providing air cover over Allied invasion forces at Anzio on 29 January 1944. (Flying Officer L.H. Baker, Royal Air Force)

included reccos of French ports such as Dieppe, Ostende and Calais; reccos of shipping along the French coast and in the English Channel; patrols of Dungeness and Hastings area; and scrambles.[64]

The dominant air superiority fighter capability of the Griffon engine powered Spitfire Mk14 was best displayed in its success as a V-1 'Buzz Bomb' interceptor and destroyer. Mk14s excelled in this role, starting with the commencement of V-1 launches against civilian targets in Britain in 1944, and quickly became the best Spitfire variant to combat this terrifying threat. A common tactic employed by Mk14 pilots was to fly alongside the V-1s in flight and, using a wingtip of their aircraft, nudge the flying bombs off course from their designated targets.

The previously shown RAF Spitfire Mk14 nudges the German V-1 off course, preventing the destruction of its target and untold loss of British civilian lives. (US National Archives, College Park, Maryland, Still Pictures Branch)

During Operation Overlord (D-Day), Supermarine Seafire Mk3s flew important aerial observation and naval fleet defence missions. In the Pacific, the Supermarine Seafire Mk2 held its own against the nimble Japanese Mitsubishi A6M5 Zero. Although it matched up well against the Zero, the Seafire Mk2's sturdier and better-armed American counterparts, the Grumman F6F Hellcat and Chance Vought F4U Corsair, fared even better against the Japanese opposition. Later versions of the Spitfire, both in RAF and Royal Australian Air Force (RAAF) service, also achieved great success in aerial combat against the Imperial Japanese Naval Air Force and the Imperial Japanese Army Air Force.

Late war Seafires excelled as Allied naval fleet defenders toward the end of the Second World War, thwarting numerous Japanese aerial kamikaze missions. The Seafires' greatest success was achieved on 15 August 1945. On that day, late war Seafires destroyed eight Japanese kamikaze aircraft. During the Korean War, Seafire Mk47s excelled in providing close air support for United Nations ground forces battling Communist North Korean and Chinese Army ground forces.

An RAF Spitfire Mk14 catches up with a German V-1 'Buzz Bomb'. (US National Archives, College Park, Maryland, Still Pictures Branch)

A captured late war Japanese Mitsubishi A6M5 Type 52 Zero undergoing flight evaluation above Naval Air Station Patuxent River, Maryland, in the United States on 25 September 1944. (US National Archives, College Park, Maryland, Still Pictures Branch)

A rear view of the captured Mitsubishi Zero. (US National Archives, College Park, Maryland, Still Pictures Branch)

A SPITFIRE ENCOUNTER WITH 'THE DEADLY FLEA', THE ROCKET-POWERED MESSERSCHMITT ME 163 KOMET

In July 1944, the RAF first encountered the rocket-powered Messerschmitt Me 163 Komet interceptor, dubbed 'The Deadly Flea'. This encounter was documented by the USAAF in its *Weekly Informational Intelligence Summary No. 72*, dated 29 July 1944:

Messerschmitt 163 vs Spitfire

(Note: The Me 163 is believed to be powered by a liquid rocket unit, which the pilot may use in short bursts to increase the endurance.)

An RAF Spitfire on reconnaissance may have encountered a Me 163 over Germany recently. Flying at 37,000 feet, the Spitfire pilot saw a white trail about 7,000 feet below him and something more than a mile horizontally. He noticed that the trail disappeared and reappeared at regular intervals as the unknown aircraft climbed toward him.

In the time that it took the British ship to climb to 41,000 feet the unknown plane climbed approximately 8,000 feet and reduced the horizontal distance to about 1,000 yards. At this point the white trails disappeared and the Spitfire returned to England.

The RAF pilot stated that the enemy plane seemed to be 'nearly all wing,' with what looked like a marked sweep-back. This tallies with previous descriptions of the Me 163.[65]

Side view of a captured rocket-powered German Messerschmitt Me 163 Komet interceptor at Wright Field in Dayton, Ohio, United States, in May 1946. (US National Archives, College Park, Maryland, Still Pictures Branch)

Front view of the Me 163 Komet interceptor at Wright Field. (US National Archives, College Park, Maryland, Still Pictures Branch)

Wing Commander A.G. Page of 125 Wing RAF embarks on a ground attack mission in his Spitfire Mk9e 'AGP'. His aircraft, wearing invasion stripes on the undersides of the wings, is armed with a 500lb GP bomb under the fuselage and two 250lb GP bombs mounted on underwing racks. Page is launching his mission from Longues, Normandy, in 1944. (Pilot Officer Saidman, RAF)

COMBAT EFFECTIVENESS OF THE SPITFIRE AS A FIGHTER-BOMBER

The Spitfire was also an exceptional tactical fighter-bomber, providing critical close air support during Allied ground offensives. In Europe, Spitfire Mk9s provided crucial close air support for Allied ground forces during the Allied advance through France following D-Day. In the Far East, Spitfires provided crucial close air support for British and Australian ground forces in Burma. In early 1945, Royal Navy Seafires played an instrumental role in the destruction of Japanese oil refineries in Sumatra.

COMBAT EFFECTIVENESS OF THE SPITFIRE AS A PHOTO-RECONNAISSANCE PLATFORM

Photo Reconnaissance (PR) Spitfires played a crucial role in ensuring Allied victory in the Second World War, from tracking the rapid German advance through Europe during the Blitzkrieg to surveying damage to large

A captured German Me 163 Komet placed on public display during the Philadelphia Air Show on 11 November 1949. (US National Archives, College Park, Maryland, Still Pictures Branch)

German dams caused by British Avro Lancaster Dambuster bombers during Operation Chastise.

Spitfires were first used as photo-reconnaissance platforms prior to and during the Blitzkrieg. These aircraft, designated as PR Mk1as, spotted the swelling wave of German ground forces and armour along Germany's borders preparing to ransack Europe. RAF Spitfire PR Mk4s played crucial roles in tracking the whereabouts of German warships that posed grave threats to Allied merchant as well as warship fleets.

One of the most important contributions that Spitfire PRs made to Allied victory in the Second World War was their role in surveying damage sustained by large dams throughout Germany during Operation Chastise, the British plan to destroy large German dams. The dams targeted were the Eder and Möhne Dams, and their destruction would flood Germany's Ruhr Valley and render its hydroelectric capability useless. The raids were carried out via RAF Bomber Command Avro Lancaster Dambuster bomber units organised by RAF Bomber Command's Guy Gibson.

RAF Bomber Command Avro Lancaster Dambuster damage to the Möhne Dam, as surveyed by Flying Officer Jerry Fray's (RAF 542 Squadron) Spitfire PR Mk11 on 17 May 1943. Note the barrage balloons strategically positioned in the air around the dam by the Germans. (Flying Officer Jerry Fray, RAF)

A vivid account of such survey work was later provided by RAF 542 Squadron Spitfire PR Mk11 pilot, Flying Officer Jerry Fray, who performed the survey flight following sunrise the day after the Möhne Dam raid:

> When I was about 150 miles from the Möhne Dam, I could see the Industrial haze over the Ruhr area and what appeared to be a cloud to the east. On flying closer, I saw that what seemed to be cloud was the sun shining on the flood waters. I looked down into the deep valley which had seemed so peaceful three days before (on an earlier reconnaissance mission) but now it was a wide torrent. The whole valley of the river was inundated with only patches of high ground and the tops of trees and church steeples showing above the flood. I was overcome by the immensity of it.[66]

In late 1943 and early 1944, RAF Spitfire PR Mk11s flew important photo-reconnaissance flights surveying V-1 sites in northern France. Photos obtained during these 'recon' flights proved to be invaluable to Allied war planners for conducting Operation Crossbow, attack missions carried out on V-1 sites in northern France. The PR Mk11's swift speed capability even attracted the attention of the USAAF, which acquired several PR Mk11s for operational use with the 14th Photo Squadron in 1944.

A MAKER OF ACES

The Spitfire was definitively a maker of aces. This was certainly the case in the exploits of the RAF's three top-scoring aces of the Second World War – Adolph Gysbert 'Sailor' Malan, Sir Douglas Robert Steuart Bader and James Edgar 'Johnnie' Johnson.

During the Battle of Britain, one of the greatest air battles ever fought, the Spitfire Mk1 made an ace out of South African, Sailor Malan. During the high point of the battle, Malan commanded RAF 74 Squadron, which first saw combat on 11 August 1940. By 12 August, the squadron tallied a total of thirty-eight German aircraft destroyed. In March 1941, Malan became the wing commander of the Biggin Hill wing, leading fighter sweeps over Nazi occupied Europe. In early 1942, he left the Biggin Hill wing and commanded a reserve wing, having amassed a final aerial victory

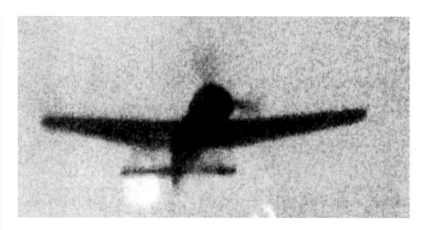

On 23 August 1943, the German Luftwaffe's Erich Borounik, piloting this Fw 190, fell victim to the guns of Johnny Johnson's Spitfire Mk9. (Royal Air Force)

Captain Adolph Gysbert 'Sailor' Malan. (Stannus, RAF)

Group Captain Douglas Robert Steuart Bader. (Mr S.A. Devon, RAF)

tally of twenty-seven enemy aircraft destroyed. Heading into 1942, Malan was Britain's highest-scoring aerial victory ace.

Following numerous highly successful combat outings flying Hawker Hurricanes during the Battle of Britain, Douglas Bader became wing commander of three RAF Spitfire Mk5b squadrons based at Tangmere, England – 145, 610 and 616 Squadrons. These Spitfire squadrons performed fighter sweeps and bomber escort duty over north-western Europe. From June–July 1941, the Spitfire Mk5a solidified Bader's position as a 'pre-eminent' RAF ace. Some of his most productive aerial ace exploits are described below.

Bader downed a Bf 109E over the water close to Desvres on 21 June 1941. He followed this action up by claiming two Bf 109F kills on 25 June 1941. He downed another Bf 109E on 4 July 1941. He later claimed an additional Bf 109 on 6 July. Bader destroyed another Bf 109 on 23 July. From 24 March 1941 to 9 August 1941, Bader performed a total of sixty-two fighter sweeps.[67]

He was shot down over Nazi occupied France on 9 August 1941, while flying a Spitfire Mk5a on a fighter sweep. He bailed out of his severely damaged Spitfire and was subsequently taken prisoner by German ground forces. He was ultimately interned as a POW at Colditz Castle, spending the remainder of the war there until being freed by the First United States Army in April 1945. Controversy as to the cause of his shooting down persists to this day.

Johnnie Johnson was one of the RAF's most successful fighter aces in the European theatre during the Second World War. Johnson racked up a kill total of thirty-four German aircraft destroyed during the war, with his last aerial victory being registered in September 1944. The thirty-four German aircraft destroyed by Johnson included fourteen Bf 109s and twenty Fw 190s. He began his combat career in the Second World War flying a Spitfire Mk1 and ended his combat career in the war flying a Spitfire Mk9. The Spitfire and Johnnie Johnson became truly formidable weapons against the German Luftwaffe in the Second World War.

EARNING THE RESPECT OF THE ENEMY

During the Battle of Britain, the Spitfire demonstrated its combat effectiveness time and again to the Germans, to the extent that even the famous German ace and future Luftwaffe general of fighters, Adolf Galland, dreamed of commanding his own squadron of Spitfires. He expressed this thought to Reichsmarshall Herman Göering during one of his visits to a Luftwaffe airfield in France when Göering inquired what Galland's greatest needs were. As stated by Galland, 'I would like an outfit of Spitfires for my squadron.'[68]

Another distinguished Luftwaffe fighter ace flying Me 109s, Günther Rall, also spoke highly of the Spitfire after the war. As stated by Rall, 'We could not use our altitude advantage nor our superiority in a dive … the Spitfire had a marvellous rate of turn, and when we were tied to the bombers and had to dogfight them, that turn was very important.'[69]

Wing Commander James E. 'Johnny' Johnson is greeted by his best friend, labrador Sally, after returning from a mission at Bazenville Landing Ground, Normandy, on 31 July 1944. Johnson's Spitfire Mk9 (background) is sporting invasion stripes on the wings. (Royal Air Force)

6

THE LEGEND LIVES

It was a true shame that R.J. Mitchell never had the opportunity to see his tremendous air superiority asset, the Supermarine Spitfire, in combat. Its legacy and legend, however, lives on in the form of refurbished Spitfires and Seafires flying at air shows and Second World War commemorations, as well as in monument displays paying tribute to both the Spitfire and its brave pilots.

EXAMPLES OF RESTORED SPITFIRES OF VARIOUS MARKS FLYING AT AIR SHOWS AND AERIAL DEMONSTRATIONS TODAY

Today, a total of fifty-five restored Spitfires dazzle audiences and onlookers at air shows and Second World War commemorative flights all over the world. Several of these are routinely flown at air shows and in the Battle of Britain Memorial Flight in England. A complete listing of flyable Spitfires/Seafires in England is as follows:

1: Spitfire F Mk1a (N3200 – Mark One Partnership LLC, owner), flies out of Duxford Airfield.

2: Spitfire F Mk1a (P9374 – Mark One Partnership LLC, owner), flies out of Duxford Airfield.

3: Spitfire F Mk1a (X4650), flies out of Duxford Airfield.

4: Spitfire F Mk1a (AR213 – Sheringham Aviation, owner).

5: Spitfire F Mk2a (P7350 – RAF Battle of Britain Memorial Flight, owner), flies out of RAF Coningsby, Lincolnshire.

6: Spitfire F Mk5b (BM597 – Historic Aircraft Collection, owner), flies out of Duxford.

7: Spitfire LF Mk5b (EP120 – The Fighter Collection, owner), flies out of Duxford.

8: Spitfire LF Mk9b (MH434 – The Old Flying Machine Company, owner), flies out of Duxford.

9: Spitfire TR9 (MJ627 – RV Aviation, owner), flies out of Goodwood Airfield.

10: Spitfire LF Mk9e (Mk356 – RAF Battle of Britain Memorial Flight, owner), flies out of RAF Coningsby, Lincolnshire.

11: Spitfire LF Mk9c (Mk912 – Peter Monk, owner), flies out of Biggin Hill, Kent.

12: Spitfire TR9 (ML407 – Carolyn Grace, owner), flies out of RAF Bentwaters, Suffolk.

13: Spitfire TR9 (PT462 – The Dragon Flight, owner), flies out of Abergele, north Wales.

14: Spitfire TR9 (PV202 – Historic Flying Ltd, owner), flies out of Duxford.

15: Spitfire HF Mk9e (RR232 – Martin Phillips, owner), flies out of Colerne, Wiltshire.

16: Spitfire TR9 (SM520 – Steve Brooks, owner), flies out of Goodwood.

17: Spitfire HF Mk9e (TA805 – Biggin Hill Heritage Hangar, owner), flies out of Biggin Hill, Kent.

18: Spitfire HF Mk9e (TD314 – Biggin Hill Heritage Hangar, owner), flies out of Biggin Hill, Kent.

19: Spitfire PR Mk11 (PL965 – Hangar 11 Collection, owner), flies out of North Weald.

20: Spitfire FR Mk14e (MV293 – The Fighter Collection, owner), flies out of Duxford.

21: Spitfire LF Mk16e (RW382 – Biggin Hill Heritage Hangar, owner), flies out of Biggin Hill, Kent.

22: Spitfire LF Mk16e (TD248 – Spitfire Ltd, owner), flies out of Duxford and Humberside.

23: Spitfire LF Mk16e (TE311 – RAF Battle of Britain Memorial Flight, owner), flies out of RAF Coningsby, Lincolnshire.

24: Spitfire FR Mk18e (SM845 – Spitfire Ltd, owner), flies out of Duxford and Humberside.

25: Spitfire PR Mk19 (PM631 – RAF Battle of Britain Memorial Flight, owner), flies out of RAF Coningsby, Lincolnshire.

26: Spitfire PR Mk19 (PS853 – Rolls-Royce plc, owner).

27: Spitfire PR Mk19 (PS915 – RAF Battle of Britain Memorial Flight, owner), flies out of RAF Coningsby, Lincolnshire.

28: Seafire F Mk17 (SX336 – Kennet Aviation, owner), flies out of North Weald, Essex.

Battle of Britain Memorial Flight Spitfire Mk5b (AB910, RF-D) takes to the skies on Kemble Air Day, 21 June 2009. (Adrian Pingstone)

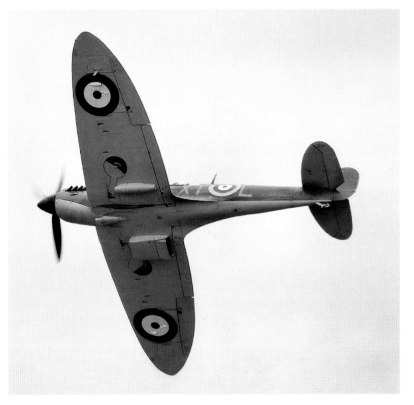

A Spitfire PR Mk11 (PL965) at the Royal International Air Tattoo, Fairford, Gloucestershire, England, in July 2008. (Adrian Pingstone)

A refurbished Spitfire Mk2a (P7350) in flight over Kemble Airport, Gloucestershire, England, on Kemble Air Day, June 2008. The aircraft, a member of the Battle of Britain Memorial Flight, is the sole remaining flyable Spitfire that participated in the Battle of Britain. (Adrian Pingstone)

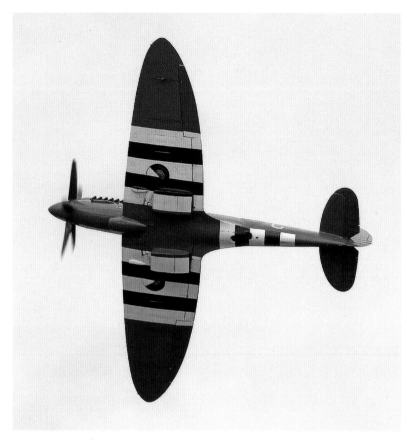

A refurbished Griffon-engined Spitfire PR Mk19 (PS853) in flight at Kemble Air Day in June 2008. (Adrian Pingstone)

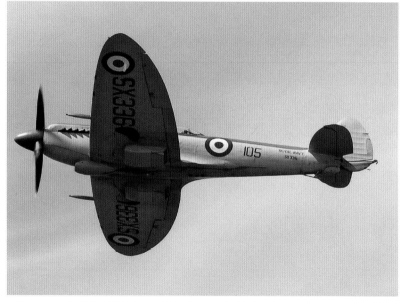

Top and bottom: Royal Navy Seafire F Mk17 SX336 heads out on a demonstration flight at the Cotswold Air Show at Cotswold Airport, Gloucestershire, England, in June 2010. (Adrian Pingstone)

A Battle of Britain Memorial Flight aircraft formation flyby, comprised of two refurbished Hawker Hurricanes and five refurbished Supermarine Spitfires, at the Duxford Airshow in May 2007. (Chickenfeed9)

An American B-17 Flying Fortress bomber, dubbed 'Sally', flies in formation with two refurbished RAF Spitfire Mk9 fighter escorts at the Memorial Day ceremony at Madingley American Cemetery, Cambridge, on 31 May 2004. (US National Archives, College Park, Maryland, Still Pictures Branch)

A Battle of Britain Memorial Flight Spitfire Mk14 on static exhibition at RAF Lakenheath, England, for the Battle of Britain ceremony held on 24 June 2000. The ceremony marked the 29th annual and last reunion of Battle of Britain flyers. A USAF F-15E Strike Eagle, based at RAF Lakenheath, can be seen in the background to the left. (US National Archives, College Park, Maryland, Still Pictures Branch)

Sqn Ldr Paul Day, Royal Air Force Memorial Flight, prepares to perform a flight demonstration in his Spitfire Mk14 at the Battle of Britain ceremony at RAF Lakenheath on 24 June 2000. (US National Archives, College Park, Maryland, Still Pictures Branch)

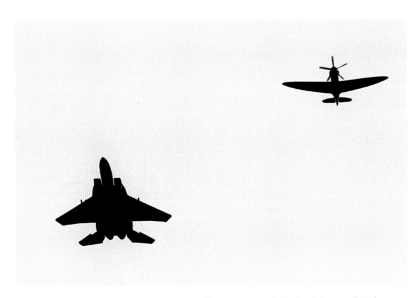

Two generations of air superiority fighters. Left: USAF F-15C Eagle of the 493rd Fighter Squadron, 48th Fighter Wing, RAF Lakenheath, England. Right: A refurbished RAF Spitfire Mk14 in flight during the Battle of Britain Memorial Flight on 24 June 2000. (US National Archives, College Park, Maryland, Still Pictures Branch)

USAF Senior Airman Christy Sapulpa-Myers, 48th Communications Squadron, 48th Fighter Wing, shoots video of the Spitfire exhibited at the Battle of Britain Park at RAF Lakenheath on 13 December 2000. (US National Archives, College Park, Maryland, Still Pictures Branch)

MONUMENTS IN TRIBUTE TO 'THE PROUD FEW'

One of the most moving monuments in England erected in tribute to 'The Proud Few' resides at the USAF AFB at RAF Lakenheath. The monument, dedicated to the brave Spitfire and Hawker Hurricane pilots during the Battle of Britain, features a full-scale Spitfire Mk5b mounted on a pedestal in flight configuration, with an engraved plaque monument positioned in front of the aircraft display. On the monument are the engraved words profoundly and emphatically proclaimed by British Prime Minister Winston Churchill following the Battle of Britain:

If the British Empire and its commonwealth last for a thousand years, men will still say, 'This was their finest hour'.

Numerous other monuments erected in tribute to 'The Proud Few' and the legendary Spitfire dot the British countryside. A sculpture, known as the *Sentinel*, of three airborne Spitfires, produced by Tim Tolkien, adorns the junction between the A47 and A452 at Castle Bromwich in Birmingham, England. The sculpture was erected in tribute to the Castle Bromwich

USAF 48th Component Repair Squadron (CRS), 48th Fighter Wing, maintenance crews wash a Spitfire Mk5 exhibited at the Battle of Britain Memorial Park at RAF Lakenheath on 20 May 2002. (US National Archives, College Park, Maryland, Still Pictures Branch)

THE FEW

THIS MEMORIAL IS DEDICATED TO THE AIRMEN OF MANY NATIONS WHO FLEW WITH THE R.A.F. DURING THE BATTLE OF BRITAIN AND SOARED INTO THE HEAVENS THAT OTHERS MIGHT LIVE

IN JULY 1940, HITLER'S LUFTWAFFE BEGAN AN AERIAL SIEGE OF ENGLAND AIMED AT DESTROYING THE ROYAL AIR FORCE IN PREPARATION FOR A CROSS CHANNEL ASSAULT BY THE GERMAN ARMY AND NAVY. OUTNUMBERED SOMETIMES FOUR TO ONE, EXHAUSTED PILOTS OF THE R.A.F. MET THE AERIAL ARMADA FLYING THOUSANDS OF SORTIES, DAY AFTER DAY, NIGHT AFTER NIGHT, TO ENSURE GREAT BRITAIN'S VERY SURVIVAL. BY THE END OF SEPTEMBER THE R.A.F. HAD INFLICTED CRIPPLING LOSSES ON THE LUFTWAFFE, DESTROYING OVER 1880 ENEMY AIRCRAFT, THEREBY FORCING HITLER TO CANCEL HIS INVASION PLANS OF THE BRITISH ISLES. ALTHOUGH FEWER IN NUMBER, THE R.A.F. LOSSES WERE DISPROPORTIONATELY HIGHER. MORE THAN 530 AIRMEN PAID THE ULTIMATE SACRIFICE, SOME EVEN RAMMING ENEMY AIRCRAFT WHEN THEIR OWN GUNS JAMMED OR AMMUNITION RAN OUT.

AFTER THE BATTLE, THE BRITISH PRIME MINISTER SIR WINSTON CHURCHILL IMMORTALIZED THOSE AIRMEN THAT FLEW DURING THE BATTLE OF BRITAIN WITH THE FOLLOWING WORDS: - IF THE BRITISH EMPIRE AND ITS COMMONWEALTH LAST FOR A THOUSAND YEARS, MEN WILL STILL SAY

"THIS WAS THEIR FINEST HOUR"

DEDICATED BY
THE BATTLE OF BRITAIN FIGHTER ASSOCIATION
AND THE 48TH FIGHTER WING
SATURDAY 12TH JULY 1997

The memorial plaque at the Battle of Britain Memorial Park, 48th Fighter Wing, RAF Lakenheath, strategically placed in tribute to the RAF Battle of Britain fliers. (US National Archives, College Park, Maryland, Still Pictures Branch)

Aircraft Factory that spewed factory-fresh Spitfires at a feverish pace from the assembly lines during the Second World War.

Another sculpture representing the Spitfire MkI prototype (K5054) was erected at the entry point of Southampton International Airport. The airport was formerly known as Eastleigh Aerodrome, where K5054 was flown for the first time in March 1936. A fiberglass Spitfire, representative of a Polish Squadron aircraft, is exhibited at RAF Northolt. Northolt is the sole remaining active-duty base that was also active during the Battle of Britain. Close to the Douglas Bader School located on Thornaby Road resides a Spitfire model permanently exhibited in tribute to the famous Second World War Spitfire pilot and RAF Thornaby, which was active during the war.

We should be proud of 'The Few' for their undefeatable bravery and sacrifice carried out against overwhelming numbers and odds during one of the most pivotal periods of the Second World War. This resilience of the human spirit displayed by 'The Few' was carried out so that others could remain free. The beautiful flying Spitfire examples and the grand monuments erected in tribute to their gallant fliers are the remaining legacy of this superb airplane that helped to save the world.

NOTES

1 RG 255, NACA Classified, Ide 1915–1949, NND 836516, 1050, Sikorsky thru Supermarine, Box 287, *Supermarine: Flying Boats, Yachts and High Speed Racing Seaplanes, the Supermarine Aviation Works Ltd, Southampton, England* (1929), Gale & Polden, LTD., Printers, Aldershot, 978.c., p.3. US National Archives at College Park, Maryland, Textual Reference Branch.

2 RG 255, NACA Classified, Ide 1915–1949, NND 836516, 1050, Sikorsky thru Supermarine, Box 287, *National Advisory Committee for Aeronautics: Supermarine 'Seal'*, prepared by Paris Office, NACA, September, 1921, p.1. US National Archives at College Park, Maryland, Textual Reference Branch.

3 RG 255, NACA Classified, Ide 1915–1949, NND 836516, 1050, Sikorsky thru Supermarine, Box 287, *Supermarine: Flying Boats, Yachts and High Speed Racing Seaplanes, the Supermarine Aviation Works Ltd, Southampton, England* (1929), Gale & Polden, LTD., Printers, Aldershot, 978.c., p.12. US National Archives at College Park, Maryland, Textual Reference Branch.

4 Holmes, Tony, *Dogfight: The Greatest Air Duels of World War II*, 'Part I: The Battle of Britain 1940, Spitfire vs Bf 109E', p.16 (New York: Chartwell Books Inc., 2013).

5 RG 255, NACA Classified, Ide 1915–1949, NND 836516, 1050, Sikorsky thru Supermarine, Box 287, *Supermarine: Flying Boats, Yachts and High Speed Racing Seaplanes, the Supermarine Aviation Works Ltd, Southampton, England* (1929), Gale & Polden, LTD., Printers, Aldershot, 978.c., p.12. US National Archives at College Park, Maryland, Textual Reference Branch.

6 Ibid., pp.12 and 14.

7 RG 255, NACA Classified, Ide 1915–1949, NND 836516, 1050, Sikorsky thru Supermarine, Box 287, Aircraft Circulars, National Advisory Committee for Aeronautics, No. 67, 'Supermarine S.5 Seaplane (British): Winner of the 1927 Schneider Cup Race, Washington, March 1928', p.1. US National Archives at College Park, Maryland, Textual Reference Branch.

8 Ibid., pp.3–9.

9 RG 255, NACA Paris Office, John J. Ide, Copies of Reports on European Aviation, 1930–1931, Box No. 5, *Report from the Technical Assistant in Europe, NACA, to the National Advisory Committee for Aeronautics, Washington DC*, 'Visits to Calshot for the Schneider Contest, September 24, 1931', pp.1–5. US National Archives at College Park, Maryland, Textual Reference Branch.

10 RG 255, NACA Classified, Ide 1915–1949, NND 836516, 1050, Sikorsky thru Supermarine, Box 287, Aircraft Circulars, National Advisory Committee for Aeronautics, No. 154: The Supermarine S6B Racing Seaplane (British), (from *Aircraft Engineering*, October 1931): 'A Low-Wing Twin Float Monoplane', Washington, December 1931, pp.1–6. US National Archives at College Park, Maryland, Textual Reference Branch.

11 RG 255, NACA Classified, Ide 1915–1949, NND 836516, 1050, Sikorsky thru Supermarine, Box 287, Aircraft Circulars, National Advisory Committee for Aeronautics, No. 154 (Supplement), 'Supplement to The Supermarine S.6.B. Racing Seaplane (British): A Low-Wing Twin-Float Monoplane', Washington, February 1932, pp.1–6. US National Archives at College Park, Maryland, Textual Reference Branch.

12 Price, Alfred, *The Spitfire Story* (London: Jane's Publishing Company Ltd, 1982, p. 109).

13 RG 255, NACA Classified File 1915–58, A100 ENGLAND thru A1000 ENGLAND, Box Number 11, *Report from the Technical Assistant in Europe,*

NACA, to the National Advisory Committee for Aeronautics, Washington, DC, 'Visit to England, June–July 1936', 3 August 1936, pp.37–8. US National Archives at College Park, Maryland, Textual Reference Branch.

14 Ibid., p.39.

15 www.spitfireperformance.com/spitfire-I.html, 'Spitfire MkI Performance Testing, Aeroplane and Armament Experimental Establishment Martlesham Heath, September 1936, Handling trials of the Spitfire K5054, Summary of Flying Qualities'.

16 RG 255, NACA Classified File 1915–58, A100 ENGLAND thru A1000 ENGLAND, Box Number 11, *Report from the Technical Assistant in Europe, NACA, to the National Advisory Committee for Aeronautics, Washington, DC,* 'Visit to England, July 1938', 22 August 1938, pp.29–32. US National Archives at College Park, Maryland, Textual Reference Branch.

17 www.spitfireperformance.com/spitfire-I.html, 'Spitfire MkI Performance Testing, Aeroplane and Armament Experimental Establishment Martlesham Heath, 6 January 1939, Spitfire K9787 Merlin II Fixed pitch wooden airscrew, Performance Trials'.

18 www.spitfireperformance.com/spitfire-I.html, 'Spitfire MkI Performance Testing, Royal Aircraft Establishment at Farnborough, June 1940, Spitfire IA K9791 with Rotol Constant Speed Propeller – Me 109 E-3 Werk-Nr 1304, Comparative trials between the Me. 109 and "Rotol" Spitfire'.

19 http://aerospace.illinois.edu/m-selig/ads/aircraft.html, 'The Incomplete Guide to Airfoil Usage', David Lednicer, Aeromechanical Solutions LLC.

20 Price, Alfred, *Spitfire: Fighter Supreme* (London: Arms and Armour Press, 1991, pp.68–9, 71).

21 Price, Alfred and Mike Spick, *Handbook of Great Aircraft of WWII* (Leicester, UK: The Promotional Reprint Company Limited, 1997, p.70).

22 Green, William, *Famous Fighters of the Second World War* (Volume One) (Garden City, New York: Doubleday and Company Inc., 1965, p.28).

23 www.spitfireperformance.com/spitfire-II.html, 'Spitfire MkIIa Performance Testing, Aeroplane and Armament Experimental Establishment at Boscombe Down, England, Spitfire II P.7280, Merlin XII. Rotol Constant Speed Airscrew-Morris Radiator, Comparative Performance Trials'.

24 www.spitfireperformance.com/spitfire-V.html, 'Spitfire Mk.V Performance Testing, Comparison of Spitfire V and Me 109 F1/2'.

25 Ibid., 'Aeroplane and Armament Experiment Establishment Boscombe Down, 29 April 1941, Spitfire Mk.VA X.4922 (Merlin XLV) Brief Performance Trials'.

26 Phillips, William H., and Joseph R. Vensel, 'National Advisory Committee for Aeronautics Wartime Report: Measurements of the Flying Qualities of a Supermarine Spitfire VA Airplane', Langley Memorial Aeronautical Laboratory, Langley Field, Va., ACR September 1942, pp.18–19, as found at www.wwiiaircraftperformance.org/NACA-Spitfire-V-Flying.pdf.

27 Morgan, Eric B., and Edward Shacklady, *Spitfire: The History* (Stamford: Key Books Ltd, 2000, p.142).

28 www.spitfireperformance.com/w3134.html. 'Spitfire Mk.V Performance Testing, Aeroplane and Armament Experimental Establishment, Boscombe Down, Spitfire V.B. W.3134. (Merlin XLV.), Brief Performance Trials, 18 June 1941'.

29 www.spitfireperformance.com/spitfire-V.html. 'Spitfire Mk.V Performance Testing, Aeroplane and Armament Experimental Establishment, Boscombe Down, 15 April 1942, Spitfire Mk.VB (Tropical) AB.320 (Merlin 45), Position error, and performance with and without a 90 gallon external overload tank'.

30 Green, William, p.34.

31 www.spitfireperformance.com/aa873.html. 'Spitfire Mk.V Performance Testing, Aeroplane and Armament Experimental Establishment, Boscombe Down, 8 March 1942, Spitfire Mk.VC A.A.873 (Merlin 45), Brief Performance and Handling Trials with 4-20m/m guns fitted'.

32 Green, William, p.34.

33 Morgan, Eric B. and Edward Shacklady, *Spitfire: The History* (Stamford: Key Books Ltd, 2000, pp.154–5).

34 'Spitfire: Simply Superb, Part Three', *Air International*, Volume 28, Number 4, April 1985, p.187.

35 Green, William, p.31.

36 Price, Alfred, *The Spitfire Story*, Revised second edition (Leicester, UK: Silverdale Books, 2002, p.150).

37 Green, William, p.31.

38 Official US Government telegram from Lt J.E. Arnoult, USAAF Materiel Command, Wright Field, Dayton, Ohio, to the Commanding General, AAF Technical School, Lowry Field, Colorado, 15 August 1944. RG 342 P26, Box 3371, RD 3890, Sarah Clark Correspondence Files. US National Archives at College Park, Maryland, Textual Reference Branch.

39 www.spitfireperformance.com/spitfire-VIII.html. 'Spitfire Mk VIII Performance Testing. RAAF Headquarters Directorate of Technical Services, Special Duties and Performance Flight, Spitfire Mk.VIII JF.934 (Merlin 66) Brief Performance Trials of a Spitfire (F) – Mk.VIII, January 1944'.

40 Ibid.

41 Green, William, p.32.

42 www.spitfireperformance.com/spitfire-IX.html. 'Spitfire Mk.IX Performance Testing. Aeroplane and Armament Experimental Establishment, Boscombe Down, 22 October 1942, Spitfire F. Mk.IX BF.274 (Merlin 61), Climb and Level Speed Performance'.

43 Ibid. 'Aircraft and Armament Experimental Establishment, Boscombe Down, 17 March 1943, Spitfire F. Mk.IX BS. 428 (Merlin 61), Level Speed Performance with and without a 500lb Bomb Fitted'.

44 Letter from Colonel H.Z. Bogert (Acting Chief, Engineering Division, USAAC) to Hap Arnold (Commanding General, USAAF), 'Spitfire IX Range Extension Project', 28 July 1944. RG 342 P26, Box 3371, RD 3890, Sarah Clark Correspondence Files. US National Archives at College Park, Maryland, Textual Reference Branch.

45 Letter from Brigadier General F.O. Carroll (Chief, Engineering Division, USAAC) to Hap Arnold (Commanding General, USAAF), 'Spitfire IX Range Extension', 16 August 1944. RG 342 P26, Box 3371, RD 3890, Sarah Clark Correspondence Files. US National Archives at College Park, Maryland, Textual Reference Branch.

46 www.spitfireperformance.com/spitfire-XII.html, 'Spitfire Mk.XII Performance. Aeroplane and Armament Experimental Establishment, Boscombe Down, 29 November 1942, Spitfire F. Mk.XII D.P.845 (Griffon IIB), Climb and Level Speed Performance and Position Error Correction'.

47 Ibid. 'Aeroplane and Armament Experimental Establishment, Boscombe Down, 4 August 1943, Spitfire F. Mk.XII D.P.845 (Griffon VI), Climb and Level Speed Performance and Position Error Correction'.

48 www.spitfireperformance.com/spitfire-XIV.html, 'Spitfire Mk.XIV Performance Testing. Vickers Armstrong Ltd., Supermarine Works, 10 September 1943, Spitfire VIII (Conversion JF319), Level Speed Tests with Griffon R.G.5.S.M. Engine 18lb/sq.in Boost Rating'.

49 Ibid. 'Aeroplane and Armament Experimental Establishment, Boscombe Down, 27 October 1943, Spitfire F.Mk.VIII (Conv) (Prototype Mk.XIV) JF319 (Griffon RG5SM), Climb and Level Speed Performed and Position Error'.

50 www.spitfireperformance.com/spitfire-21.html, 'Spitfire F. Mk.21 Performance Testing. Vickers Armstrong Ltd. Supermarine Works, 27 May 1943, Spitfire F. Mark21-Griffon 61, Performance Tests of Prototype DP.851'.

51 Ibid. 'Vickers Armstrong Ltd Supermarine Works, 10 September 1943, Spitfire F.21-2nd Prototype PP.139, Brief Level Speed Tests'.

52 Rendall, Ivan, *Spitfire: Icon of a Nation* (New York: Metro Books, 2008, p.249).

53 Green, William, p.35.

54 www.spitfireperformance.com/seafireIIc.pdf, 'Spitfire Performance Testing – Seafire MkIIC. Aeroplane and Armament Experimental Establishment, Boscombe Down, Seafire IIc. M.A.970 (Merlin 46), October 1942, Climb and Level Speed Performance with and without a 30 Gallon External Fuel Tank Fitted'.

55 www.spitfireperformance.com/mb138.html, 'Spitfire Performance Testing – Seafire L. MkIIC. Aircraft and Armament Experimental Establishment, Boscombe Down, Seafire L. Mk.IIC M.B.138 (Merlin 32), 24 February 1943, Climb and Level Speed Performance'.

56 www.spitfireperformance.com/lr765.html, 'Spitfire Performance Testing – Seafire MkIII. Aircraft and Armament Experimental Establishment, Boscombe Down, Seafire III L.R.765 (Merlin 50), 11–17 August 1943, Climb and Level Speed Performance Tests on First Production Aircraft'.

57 RG 255 NACA Classified File, 1915–58, Project Number NND 917643, Box 507, Aircraft and Armament Experimental Establishment, Boscombe Down, 'Seafire F. Mk.XV NS.487 (Griffon VI), Handling Trials Including Determination of Aftmost Acceptable Centre of Gravity Position', March 1944. US National Archives at College Park, Maryland, Textual Reference Branch.

58 www.spitfireperformance.com/seafire47.pdf, 'Spitfire Performance Testing – Seafire Mk47. Naval Air Fighting Development Unit, Central Fighter Establishment, RAF West Raynham, Trial Report: Interim Report on Seafire 47 – General Service Trials, 24 May 1949'.

59 RG 255 NACA Classified File, 1915–58, Project Number NND 917643, Box 507, Aircraft and Armament Experimental Establishment, Boscombe Down, 'Spitfire IX BS.139 (Merlin 61), Spitfire Vs.AA.937 & A.B.186 (Merlin 45 and 46), and Spitfire XIIs EN.221 & EN.222 (Griffon IIB), The effect of 'Clipping' Spitfire Wings', by Flt Lt D.R.H. Dickinson/.F.R.Ae.S. US National Archives at College Park, Maryland, Textual Reference Branch.

60 www.spitfireperformance.com/freeborn-24-5-40.jpg, 'Spitfire Performance Testing – Spitfire MkI. P/O John Freeborn, Combat Report, 24 May 1940'.

61 www.spitfireperformance.com/Webster-29july40.jpg, 'Spitfire Performance Testing – Spitfire MkI. F/Lt John Webster – 41 Sqn, Combat Report, 29 July 1940. Archives of M. Williams'.

62 www.spitfireperformance.com/gribble-12lbs.jpg, 'Spitfire Performance Testing – Spitfire MkI. F/Lt George Gribble, 54 Sqn, Combat Report, 15 August 1940'.

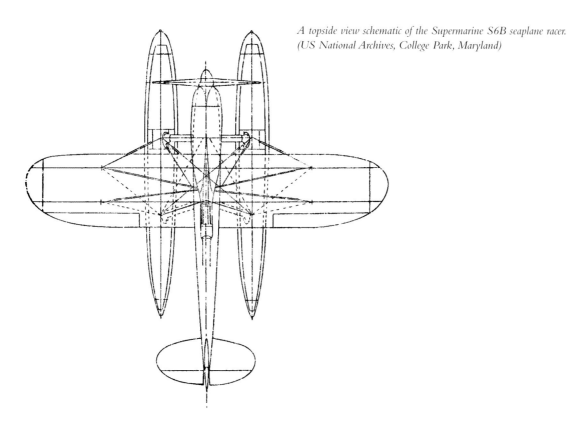

A topside view schematic of the Supermarine S6B seaplane racer.
(US National Archives, College Park, Maryland)

63 www.spitfireperformance.com/no64spit9.jpg, 'Spitfire Performance Testing – Spitfire MkIX. 64 Squadron Operational with Spitfire IXs (Supplemental), 28 July 1942'. Archives of M. Williams.

64 www.spitfireperformance.com/spitfire-XII.html, 'Spitfire Performance Testing – Spitfire MkXII. Spitfire Mk XII Performance – Brief Operational History'. Written by Mike Williams and Neil Stirling.

65 'Weekly Informational Intelligence Summary No. 72, 29 July 1944'. Office of the Intelligence Officer, Headquarters, Air Service Command, p.3. Microfilm IRIS Ref: A2203, Frame: 1675, US Department of the Air Force, Air Force Historical Research Agency, Maxwell Air Force Base, Alabama.

66 Foggo, Daniel and Michael Burke, 'I captured proof of Dambusters' raid', *Sunday Telegraph*, 15 January 2001. Retrieved 1 February 2008.

67 Lucas, Laddie, *Flying Colours: The Epic Story of Douglas Bader* (London: Hutchinson Publishing Group, 1981, p.179).

68 Rendall, Ivan, p.170.

69 Ibid.

INDEX